Jean Pierre Aulneau

The Aulneau Collection, 1734-1745

Jean Pierre Aulneau

The Aulneau Collection, 1734-1745

ISBN/EAN: 9783337218263

Printed in Europe, USA, Canada, Australia, Japan

Cover: Foto ©Lupo / pixelio.de

More available books at **www.hansebooks.com**

I

RARE
— OR —
UNPUBLISHED DOCUMENTS.
II

THE
AULNEAU COLLECTION
1734-1745.

EDITED
— BY THE —
REV. ARTHUR E. JONES,
OF THE SOCIETY OF JESUS.

MONTREAL.
ARCHIVES OF ST. MARY'S COLLEGE
1893.

UNPUBLISHED DOCUMENTS

RELATING TO

CATHOLIC CANADIAN HISTORY.

THE AULNEAU LETTERS.

1734-1745.

NTIL 1890 little or nothing was known of Father Jean (?) Pierre Aulneau, even among the few who devote their time to Canadian or American historical researches, save that a Jesuit of the name of Aulneau was massacred in company with De LaVerandrye's son, at the Lake of The Woods, in the beginning of June, 1736. The unexpected discovery of a number of letters written by or relating to the Father has awakened a new interest in the matter.

During the Advent of 1889, Fathers Dauchez, Lallemand and Legall, of the Society of Jesus, were engaged giving a mission in Vendée, France. The result was very consoling. About six hundred men—a large number for the place—received on Christmas morning at the close of the exercises. Among the latter was the venerable descendant of the ancient family of the Aulneaus. Previous to this he had never had any intercourse with the members of the Jesuit order. He informed them, however, that a number of old letters had been passed down as an heirloom in the family from father to son. They dated over 150 years back. From them it appeared that formerly a member of his family had been put to death by the Indians in the wilds of North America. He kindly allowed them to be copied, and moreover furnished several interesting details relating to Father Aulneau hitherto unknown.

The present representative of the Aulneau family, and possessor of these letters, resides at his country seat at Bournezeau, Vendée. He explains that this historical treasure escaped destruction during the Vendean wars, when so many other historical relics were pillaged or destroyed by the revolutionary hordes, owing to the fact that the Aulneau manor was the headquarters of the Vendean staff. His son, Monsieur Paul Aulneau, is at present " Conseiller Général de Vendée."

It is the translation of this collection which was first published in the CANADIAN MESSENGER, we now offer to the general public ; and it should be borne in mind that these letters have not yet appeared in print in the original French.

Father Aulneau was born April 21, 1705, at Moutiers-sur-le-Hay, in Vendée, for it was there that the manor of the Aulueaus or Seigneurs de la Touche was situated. His brother Jean Baptiste was born December 15, 1709. His brother Charles was also a Jesuit, and his sister Thérèse was a nun of the "Union Chrétienne de Fontenoy;" she enteied religion in 1730 and died in 1779. He had still another brother Michael, whose health was always weak. He became a Sulpician, and entered at Angers in 1734. He was born in 1716 and died at Autuŋ in 1752.

Our missionary embarked at La Rochelle, May 29, 1734, on board the "Ruby," commanded by the chevalier Chaon. Mgr. Dosquet, fourth Bishop of Quebec, had taken passage on the same vessel with a number of re-cruits to fill vacancies in the ranks of his diocesan clergy. There were also ou board three priests of St. Sulpice, whose names are not given, but who, we have reason to believe, were Jean Charles Chevalier, François Piquet and Pierre Sartelon.

Several other Jesuit missionaries sailed for Canada with Father Aulneau. Father Pierre de Lauzon, superior general of the Canadian missions, who had gone to France in quest of new evangelical labors, was returning with Luc François Nau, Jean de La Pierre, and, in all probability, also with Barthelemi Galpin, priests of the Society of Jesus. Besides these there was a large number of sailors and soldiers—for the "Ruby" was a man-of war—one hundred new recruits for the King's posts in the colony, and eighty smugglers, who had already languished a year in prison, but of whom, no doubt, the colonial authorities were expected to make honest citizens. The latter were in a semi-nude and filthy condition ; and if the vessel's gun-room, which served as a sleeping cabin for all, was crowded to suffocation, its living cargo was as nothing when compared to the parasitical stow-aways which swarmed on the limbs and clothing of this motley crew of contrabandists. Little wonder then if after forty-seven days of a rough navigation the pest should break out among the passengers and sailors huddled together as they were within the stifling hold. Father Aulneau, in his letters, is silent on his own self-sacrifice in laboring among the sick to alleviate their bodily sufferings and in bringing peace to their souls ; but Father Nau tells us how the future victim of Indian cruelty devoted himself without intermission to so repulsive a duty.

He escaped, however, serious illness until he reached Quebec. Brother Jean Jard Boispineau came down as far as Cape Maillard in a launch to meet the ship, and took on board Father Aulneau, who already showed the premonitory symptoms of the dread disease. After three days he was prostrated with the fever, and twice was at the point of death. God reserved him, however, for a different kind of sacrifice. Brother Boispineau, the skill-

ful infirmarian, who according to the records of the time
saved on different occasions so many other precious
lives, treated him successfully, and by careful nursing
restored him to perfect health.

Father Aulneau had landed on the 12th of August.
The man-of-war, with the other passengers on board,
reached Quebec only on the 16th, after a disastrous
passage of eighty days, twenty men having been carried
off by the contagion.

As soon as he had regained sufficient strength he began
his fourth year of theology, and he was very likely directed
in his studies by Father François Bertin Guesnier, whose
health, never robust, was fast giving away under his
many duties self imposed and allotted by obedience. He
was a man of about forty but deeply versed in theological science, which he had taught since his arrival in
Quebec in the summer of 1732. But what was of far
more importance to Father Aulneau, he was eminently a
man of prayer, animated with an untiring zeal in God's
service and relentless in the practice of self-denial and
mortification.

The young missionary found in him a kindred spirit ;
and though he saw much to admire in the other more
venerable missionaries around him, he nevertheless took
Father Guesnier more especially as his model. He was
indeed an example to him in the perfect observance of
all religious practices, but he was to set him the example
in that all-important act which saints make their study
throughout a lifetime, that of passing from time to
eternity.

Father Guesnier's obituary, written in October, 1735,
by his superior, Father Pierre de Lauzon, is the true
delineation of a saint. It will be reproduced in its proper
place. We shall quote here but one passage : " He
employed his last days in continually uniting his own

dispositions with those of our Saviour during His agony and while on the cross. The morning of his demise he had the office of the dead recited for him, and he passed to a better life tenderly kissing the crucifix and with his dying lips pressed to the wound of the Sacred Heart of Jesus, for which he had a particular devotion." This death, precious in the sight of God, took place on December 18, 1734.

Father Aulneau counted it a happiness to have been called upon to watch during two nights at the bedside of his fellow-religious, and the sight of his holy death encouraged him to give himself up still more unreservedly to the service of his Master.

Winter at last wore away, and with the opening of navigation he set out for Montreal. On the 13th of June he left the latter town, to spend a few days at Sault St. Louis ; and finally, on the 21st of the same month, three weeks after Pentecost, he began his long journey towards Fort St. Charles and the Lake of the Woods. On July 27, 1735, he wrote to Father Nau from Michilimackinac, but the letter is missing from the collection. He reached Fort St. Charles on October 23, whence he wrote his last letter to Father Bonin, in France, and in it he sets forth his projected plans for the exploration of the regions still further west. They were never carried out ; God had ordained it otherwise.

No. 1.

(*Translation.*)

FATHER AULNEAU TO HIS MOTHER.

Quebec, October 10, 1734.

MY DEAREST MOTHER,

On taking leave of you I promised to write to you as often as it would be possible for me, and to inform you of whatever would take place during my journey, and even of what might happen later on. It is with pleasure that I now begin to fulfill my promise, and this is the first letter I write since my arrival in Canada.

We embarked on the 29th of May, at two in the afternoon. Adverse winds obliged us to lie in the roadstead the 30th, so that it was only on the 31st, at three o'clock in the morning, the wind having become favorable, that we weighed anchor and set sail. We lost sight of the shores of France that same day, and we made such headway that all on board began already to congratulate themselves at the prospect of a short voyage across. Their satisfaction was but short-lived, as contrary winds soon set in ; we consoled ourselves, however, with the hope that they would not last. The sequel convinced us but too well that our hopes were vain. We took forty-seven days to reach the great Banks of Newfoundland, and during that long run, with the exception of a few days of calm, we encountered fierce head winds from the northwest, which more than once forced us to let the vessel scud before the gale. Mass was not celebrated on board either on Pentecost, or the Octave, or on Saint Peter and Saint. Paul's day, as the storm was so violent and the rolling and pitching of the ship so heavy that it was impossible to stand. Our rations on those days were biscuits and dry bread, of which each one secured a supply as best he could.

The pleasure we experienced the morrow of our arrival on the Great Banks, watching the sailors fishing for cod, compensated us for our late fatigues. In less than two hours the crew caught more than two hundred. Some were salted and the remainder distributed amongst those on board. That same day they were served up at table, and were much relished by some, others found them very insipid, myself amongst the number.

Once on the Banks, we began to catch sight of different varieties of birds which I do not think are to be seen in Europe. The kind of most frequent occurrence the sailors called "Tongeux"; it is a bird shaped somewhat like a goose, and nearly as large. Its breast is pure white, and the tips of the wings black. We saw also numbers of "Happefoix," "Godes" and "Pelyngoins." They are kinds of small duck which never abandon the vicinity of the Grand Bank.

There arose, during the night which followed our catch of codfish, a dense fog accompanied by a breeze strong enough to enable us to set sail. We therefore got under way, and began beating about as we had done heretofore. We sailed at haphazard ; and if the fog had held out an hour or two longer, a misfortune would have befallen us, for after tacking about for twenty-four hours in the darkness we were surprised when the mist cleared away to see land about a league and a half distant. It was the island of Newfoundland whose coasts loomed up high before us. We had drifted imperceptibly with the current towards the island, and found ourselves at the entrance of Placencia Bay, an English settlement and the capital of the island. We immediately put about and took a whole day to beat out from land. As soon as we thought that we were at a safe distance we continued our run along "Cavert" Bank.* It is a bank of sand about fifteen leagues long, where also large quantities of codfish are caught. We did not stop, however, to fish for any ; but what delayed us was another fog which rose, and forced us for three entire days to beat about Cavert Bank.

Meanwhile a great many on board had fallen sick, and seeing the winds always unfavorable, our officers began to grow despondent, and thought seriously of put-

---

*Cap Vert, at present Green Bank.

ting in to Louisburg, a town on "Ile Royale" (Cape Breton), which belongs to the French, and is situated at the entrance of the Gulf of the River St. Lawrence. Had they done so we should have been obliged to take shipping in some smaller craft to make the two hundred leagues which yet remained to cover before we could reach Quebec. Providentially, the winds having become a little more favorable, the officers abandoned the project, and finally determined to go as far as that port. We consequently entered the Gulf of the St. Lawrence, leaving on our left Ile Royale and St. Paul's, and on our right the islands of St. Pierre.

It was at about this date that we began to notice frequently on our masts and yard arms a kind of bird called the Cardinal, very likely because its plumage is red with the exception of the tail and the tips of the wings. It is about as large as a chaffinch, but its beak resembles that of a parrot. Several were captured by the sailors, and caged.

It was also about this time that we had to change our fore-top mast, which was split in the late gales. In spite of these delays we made some headway towards the mouth of the St. Lawrence, but before reaching it we witnessed a spectacle which, I am sure, many in Europe would set down as a pure invention. In the middle of the Gulf are two small islands, the larger of which might be about a half league in circumference. They are not named without reason Bird Islands. Never in all my life did I see as great a number as was to be seen on these islands, though they are completely denuded of trees. The ground was actually alive with them and the sky darkened. It was one of the kinds of bird of which I spoke to you above. Our captain fired a cannon ball twice in their direction as we passed, but as we were not near enough, both fell short of their mark. During the remainder of our journey up the Gulf we caught sight of Brion and Magdalen Islands (to the southwest of the Bird Islands). Porpoises of a prodigious size, whales, blowers and sea-cows awakened if they did not entirely satisfy our curiosity. Finally we reached the mouth of the river two months after leaving France. We entered it on the south side, with the Island of Anticosti on our right. The river here is more than 40 leagues wide, and is one of the greatest and most beautiful of the world. The wind soon obliged us to bear away from the southern towards the northern shore, which is of the two the less dangerous. Both are formed of very lofty mountains which extend along the river almost as far as Quebec. For several days we struggled on against the violence of the winds, which tossed us about even more boisterously than they had done heretofore, but finally made an island lying midway in the stream and which bears the name of Isle Verte. A dead calm succeeded when we were abreast of the island, and this gave us an opportunity of sending a boat ashore in quest of refreshments of which we stood in great need, as for many days we had lived on nothing but salt beef, while the number on the sick list had considerably increased. Since we left the Grand Bank, five had died and were buried at sea. The boat which we had despatched to the southern shore,—for the settlements begin about here,—took a day and a half to make her little trip, and when she again joined us we had already been two or three hours under sail, the wind having sprung up again while she was away seeking fresh provisions. She brought back but a small supply, but what little she did bring was received with satisfaction by all on board. We proceeded on our way with more caution and dread than ever, for, though we had escaped many dangers already, we had still greater ones to guard against.

We shortly made for another island which bears the name

of Ile-aux-Coudres. Near this island there is a whirlpool which makes it the most dangerous spot throughout all the passage from France to Canada. It was there that we realized for the first time that we were in summer, for since our departure from France we had experienced all along wintry weather. The sick aboard had suffered much from it. I can say that in all my experience I never endured such intense heat.

We rode at anchor two days near the whirlpool without being able to pass it, as we were wind-bound. This delay brought us a further supply of fresh provisions ; it gave us also a chance to admire at our leisure the snow-white porpoises and numbers of seal. At last a northeast wind sprung up about two o'clock in the afternoon, and we successfully cleared the whirlpool, but again cast anchor two or three leagues beyond.

On the morrow we proceeded as far as the cape called Maillard, and there I left the King's vessel. From the time we reached the whirlpool I had suffered from violent headaches, and this led Father Superior to apprehend that I had caught the ship-fever. He therefore bade me take to the launch which a Jesuit had brought down from Quebec to receive those among us who might be ailing. But fifteen leagues remained to reach that port. The evening of the day on which I left the ship I supped at the Island of Orleans, and travelling all night I arrived the following morning at six o'clock in the bark canoe which, to journey more expeditiously, we had taken at the Island of Orleans. I had up to this enjoyed good health,. I had not even been seasick during the passage across,. though it had taken us seventy-five days. Three days after landing at Quebec I was taken down with ship-fever. Twice did it bring me to death's door, but, thank God, I have now quite recovered.

Beg the Father of Mercy, my dear mother, to grant me·

the grace of devoting to His service my health and my
life which He has restored to me, and that I may bring
the poor Indians also to serve and love Him. I have
already seen a few of almost all the tribes, and there is no
more repulsive sight, but they have been ransomed by the
blood of a God. How happy shall I be if He deigns to
make use of so unworthy an instrument as myself to
bring them to love and adore Him in spirit and in truth.

I am to spend the winter in Quebec. It is a town
perched on the top of a mountain. There are houses
pretty enough, but they are built, to some extent at least,
as necessity required, without order or symmetry. The
Island of Orleans, the environs of Quebec, and either
shore, for a stretch of more than a hundred leagues
beyond, are under very good cultivation, and with the
exception of wine everything that is found in France
may be found here.

Once more, my dear mother, implore Our Lord that I
may have the grace to draw profit from the grand exam-
ples of virtue which I have before my eyes. I am here
in a college made up of former missionaries who have
sacrificed their health and strength to win for Him the
love of souls. Father Nau, who is in excellent health,
sends his compliments.

I am, my dear mother, with the tenderest affection for
now and for life,

Your servant and son,

AULNEAU, J.

No. 2.*

(Translation.)

QUEBEC, Oct. 10, 1734.

Reverend Father,—Pax Christi—

I received your letter of June 21st, and I could have experienced no pleasure greater than that which it caused me. But as you give me in it so many proofs of affection, so much practical spiritual advice, and impart such good news, that I really think any other, even less attached to your person than I am, would not have experienced less pleasure than I did.

I can assure you that I am determined to neglect nothing which might induce you to continue your correspondence.

You wish me to give you a detailed account of the in-cidents of my voyage. There is nothing I can refuse my elder brother, but you will find in it very little to interest you. One point may perhaps excite your sympathy and affect you : and that is, that it was near proving fatal to me and near being my last.

We had no mass on board on Whitsunday, nor on the octave, nor on the feast of St. Peter, for the storm was so violent that it was not possible to keep our feet on the vessel, or to take two steps without serious risk for life or limb.

You can easily imagine that under similar circumstances no fire was lit in the galley, and our repast was limited to a few slices of bread, of which luckily we had laid by a provision. We did not enjoy even this frugal

---

* Draught of an unfinished letter, without address, which Father Aulneau evidently intended for Father Charles Aulneau, S.J., his brother, completing the narrative of his passage across the Atlantic.

fare without being rudely shaken, or without danger of being thrown against each other, in spite of every possible precaution.

It was about the time when we reached the Grand Bank that our desire to see extraordinary creatures, not to be met with in Europe, was in part gratified.........

Meanwhile we had more than sixty suffering from sickness, while our officers were fairly wearied out struggling against headwinds. We had scarcely any water or provisions left. All that, was a cause of worry to Mr. de Chaon, our captain, and he was nearly giving up all hope even this time of reaching Canada. A stiff wind, which sprang up the day after our fishing incident, and which was not more favorable than the winds which had preceded it, gave him further matter for reflection. To cap the climax, this wind was accompanied by a fog so dense that we could not see each other the length of the ship.

It finally cleared away, and providentially for us, for, carried out of our course by the currents, we were on the point of being dashed upon the Newfoundland coast. We were but a league and a half away when we caught sight of land, a huge cape at the entrance of Placentia Bay, and which is called " Chapeau Rouge " (Red Cap).

Our officers were now more worried than ever, and seriously contemplated abandoning their voyage to Quebec, and of putting in rather at Louisburg, a town on Ile Royale (Cape Breton) at no great distance. This gave us great concern, as we would have been obliged to wait a long time at the island before finding a vessel to take us as far as Quebec. Providence permitted that we should experience no greater inconvenience than our apprehension, as a favorable wind which sprang up put an end to the project of landing at Louisburg.

We were none the less forced to beat about (on Cavert Bank) for two days on account of a fog, even denser than the former, which prevented our knowing whither we were:

going. All this useless tacking about was the occasion
of a visit which kept alive our curiosity for a few moments :
it was of a bird from Newfoundland, called the Cardinal ; one of the sailors captured it on the main-yard and
brought it to Mr. de Chaon.

We entered at last the Gulf of the St. Lawrence, leaving on our right the islands of St. Peter, and on our left
Ile Royale and the islands of St. Paul and St. John.
Four days were spent in traversing it, for the wind soon
ceased to be favorable.

When we had left Bird Island astern, we descried two
others, one named Brion and the other Magdalen Island.
They tell me that every year several small craft from
Quebec resort thither to capture " loup-marin " (a kind
of seal) and sea cows to be found there in great numbers.
On the evening of the fourth day after entering the Gulf,
we came in sight of the " Table-à-Rolland " and Gaspé.
The former is a cape and the latter a rather commodious
bay on the southern shore of the River St. Lawrence. We
entered the river on the morrow, sailing along the South
shore with a good wind, and having on our right the Island
of Anticosti. . Our course along this shore of the river
was of no great duration. A gale from the north-west, and
more violent than anything we had experienced since the
beginning of our voyage, forced us to beat across to the
north shore, which is less dangerous, affording us an
opportunity of reconnoitring the Seven Islands, whither
the members of the Beaver Company send every year an
agent to traffic with the Indians. We had a chance also
of seeing the Ile-aux-Œufs (Egg Island) on which the
English fleet was stranded.*

* An English admiral, Sir Hovenden Walker, in 1711, sailed from
Boston with eighty-four vessels and 9,500 men, with the intention of
wresting Quebec from the French. On August 11, 1711, part of his
fleet was wrecked off Ile-aux-Œufs ; he returned with the remaining
vessels, and in 1715 was dismissed the service. He prepared a report
of his expedition in 1720, and died in 1725,

All this was not of a nature to console us much, and we would much rather have had a favorable wind to help us along a little faster, and enable us to pass the " Battures de la Trinité " (Trinity Shoals) and those of Manikoagan, not very far off, which are two dangerous passages. But we were doomed to reach Quebec only by dint of hard tacking, and after having covered twice the distance we should have sailed had we met with less unfavorable winds.

It was therefore after repeated stretches only that we weathered these two shoals and made once more for the south shore. The worst of it was, and it worried us more than all the rest, there were no longer men enough to work the ship. Sailors and soldiers were nearly all down with the fever and unable to do duty. However, the ship had to be put about and the belaying shifted from side to side nearly every hour of the day. In the sad plight in which we were you may may conjecture that the passengers did what they could, and that we were not the most backward in hauling taut and bracing the sheets. The officers themselves set us more than once the example, and we willingly lent them a hand as we best knew how.

Finally after endless toil, ranging along the southern shore, we made the anchorage at Ile-Verte. It was about a league from this island that we cast anchor for the first time. A day of calm which succeeded enabled us to make a study of the " loups-marins " and white porpoises, and especially of the awe-inspiring mountain ranges which flank both the north and south shore of the river, stretching from its mouth far away towards Quebec.

We here received the visit of two Micmac Indians from Father Laure's mission.* Our captain kindly

* In 1889, Father Peter Laure's hitherto unpublished Relation appeared in print. It covers about forty-five closely printed octavo pages, and extends from the year 1720 to 1730. A short biography

2

greeted and feasted them, and made them a present of a supply of powder and shot before taking leave of them.

You may suppose that I scanned them with attention ; they were the first of the aborigines I had set eyes on, and I assure you I hoped never to meet with more uncleanly specimens. The great number I met with afterwards at Quebec undeceived me.

Ile-Verte is uninhabited, but on the mainland to the south there are one or two French families. M. de Chaon sent a launch to their settlements for meat and other fresh provisions. It did not return before we had set sail, wishing to take advantage of a favourable breeze which had sprung up and make the Ile-aux-Coudres. We did not succeed that day in accomplishing this, as the wind fell, so we anchored off Ile-aux-Lièvres (Hare Island), a little to the east of several large rocks which form as many islands midway in the river, and which are called the Pilgrims. The delay enabled the launch to overtake us. Its supply of fresh provisions was scanty, but what little it did bring was hailed with satisfaction by all, and gave some relief to the sick, whose number had considerably increased.

On the morrow we took advantage of a few puffs of

of the missionary serves as an introduction. F. Laure was born at Orleans, France, Sept. 17, 1688, and entered the Society of Jesus, Oct. 29, 1707. He was but a scholastic when he landed in Canada in 1711, and taught in the Jesuit college at Quebec until 1717, when he entered upon his theological course. Mgr. St. Valier ordained him a priest, at the General Hospital, Quebec, June 23, 1719. In 1720, he was assigned by his superior, Father de la Chasse, to the Saguenay missions. The field of his missionary labor extended from the Ile-aux-Coudres downwards along the north shore of the St. Lawrence to beyond the Seven Islands, and northward to the region about Lake St. John. The Micmac Indians, mentioned by Father Aulneau, did not properly belong to Father Laure's mission ; but detached parties landed sometimes at the stations belonging to it.

Father Laure died at the "Eboulements," Nov. 22, 1737.

wind to reach Ile-aux-Coudres, where we cast anchor a
few hundred yards from the famous whirlpool, the most
dangerous pass in all the river.

Here again we had an opportunity of adding to our
stock of fresh provisions, for we were weather-bound for
two days at our moorings. Towards evening, on the
third day from our arrival, we managed to pass the whirl.
pool without mishap, and the next day we succeeded in
reaching Cape Maillard.

We were now but fourteen or fifteen leagues from Quebec. By order of Father de Lauzon * I completed my
journey partly in a launch Brother Boispineau † had
come down in, and partly in a bark canoe.

I finally landed in Quebec at six in the morning of the
12th of August, seventy-five days from the time I embarked. There, Reverend Father, you have the rather
prosy particulars of my voyage. As for incidents between
decks, neither did I nor my brother Jesuits meet with any
but agreeable ones. All the officers showed us marked
attention and even real friendship, and with the excep-

---

* Counting Father Pierre Biard's administration from 1611 to 1614,
at Port-Royal and St. Sauveur, and the two administrations respect-
ively of Fathers Jerome Lalemant, François Le Mercier and Claude
Dablon, Father Pierre de Lauzon was the 21st General Superior of
the Jesuit Missions within the present limits of the Dominion. His
term of office extended from September, 1732 to 1739. He was a native
of Poitiers, France, and was born Sept. 26, 1687. He entered the Society of Jesus, Nov. 24, 1702, and came to 'anada in 1716. He died at
Quebec, Sept. 5, 1742, and belonged to the Province of Aquitaine.

† There were two coadjutor brothers of the name, both infirmarians,
attached to the college in Quebec. Jean Jard Boispineau, born at
Lamothe, diocese of Poitiers, Sept. 10, 1689. He entered the Society,
Aug. 10, 1711, and took his first vows at Quebec, Nov. 4, 1713, and his
last, Feb. 2, 1721. He died at Quebec in 1744.

Charles was the name of the younger. Born also at Lamothe, he
entered the Society Sept. 14, 1719, and took his first vows at Quebec,
Sept. 14, 1721, and his last Feb. 2, 1730. He died Jan. 30, 1760.

tion of Father de La Pierre, * we all enjoyed good health, though we moved about among two hundred fever stricken or convalescent patients. From time to time, it is true, a few little stirring events took place in the gun-room, where we were all huddled together, but as we took no active part in them, and treated them as so many jokes, I shall not speak of them.

We helped the sick as best we could, and always lived in perfect good-fellowship with the other passengers, especially with the three gentlemen of St. Sulpice, who edified us extremely by their zeal and care of the sick ; this act of charity was the cause of all but the death of two of them.

I was in hopes that once we had reached Quebec I should be rid of the headaches which began troubling me shortly before I left the vessel, and which had determined Father de Lauzon to make me take to the launch ; but the day after the feast of the Assumption (Notre Dame d'Août), date of the arrival of the ship before Quebec with the other Jesuits who had remained on board, I was taken down with the fever, and in less than five days was at death's door. Thanks to Brother Boispineau's treatment, and more than all else thanks to the prayers of our Fathers who made a novena for me, I escaped. I had a relapse, however, eight days after, which last attack was more serious than the former. I am at last, thank God, once more in the enjoyment of good health. Beg our Lord that I may expend that health and strength He has restored to me in making the poor Indians love and serve Him.

I am to pass the winter here in Quebec, and in the spring am to set out, they say, for the Sioux, provided....

---

* Father Jean de La Pierre was born at Vannes, France, Feb. 18, 1704 ; he entered the Society, March 20, 1724, as a member of the Province of France, and landed in Canada, as we have seen, Aug. 16, 1734. He returned to France in 1747.

No. 3.*

(Translation.)

FATHER LUKE FRANCIS NAU TO REV. FATHER RI-
CHARD, PROV. OF THE PROVINCE OF GUYENNE,
AT BORDEAUX.

Reverend Father,—Pax Christi—

We embarked, May 29, on the Ruby, under the command of Mons. le Chevalier de Chaon, and we remained two days in the harbor waiting for favorable winds. For that matter, these two days were quite sufficient to give us a foretaste of the tediousness of our voyage. The mere sight of the gun-room (la Ste. Barbe) was a revelation for all, but for me more than the others.

It is a room about the size of the Rhetoric class-room at Bordeaux, where a double row of frames were swung up, and which were to serve as beds for the passengers, subaltern officers and the gunners.

---

* Little is known of Father Luc François Nau, save what may be gleaned from the *Aulneau Collection*. His native place, the date of his birth and that of his entrance into the Society have not yet been determined ; but he belonged to the province of Aquitaine. He reached Quebec on August 16, 1734, as he himself informs us. He toiled, as missionary, at Sault St. Louis (Caughnawaga), from 1735 to 1743. There he received from the Iroquois the name of *Hateriata*.

At Quebec, February 2, 1738, he took the four vows of the professed fathers. Father Lauzon officiated, and Father Barthélemi Galpin and Nicolas de Gonnor witnessed the act.

He was present at Quebec at the arrival of Father Pierre Potier, Oct. 1, 1743, and his last letter from Canada to Madame Aulneau was dated from that place on Oct. 17 of the same year. He was then completely broken down in health, almost helpless from gout and threatened with loss of sight. He mentions that he is to return to France as soon as other missionaries arrive. His name no longer appears in the catalogue of Canadian missionaries of 1746, while from a letter of Charles Aulneau to his mother,—

We were packed into this dismal and noisome hold like so many sardines in a barrel. We could make our way to our hammocks only after sustaining sundry bumps and knocks on limbs and head.

A sense of delicacy forbade our disrobing, and our clothes, in time, made our backs ache. The rolling and pitching loosened the fastenings of our hammocks and hopelessly entangled them. On one occasion I was pitched out sprawling on a poor Canadian officer. It was quite a time before I could extricate myself from ropes and counterpane; meanwhile the officer had scarcely breath enough left to give vent to his profanity.

After the very first day's experience of the Ste. Barbe (the gun-room) one of the missionaries broke down, and Reverend Father de Lauzon began to fear that if we were obliged, by the rough weather, to go ashore, the disconsolate man could never bring himself to set foot on board again.

Another disagreeable feature was the company we were thrown in with day and night.............. We shunned them as much as possible, and banded together with three priests of St. Sulpice, men of intelligence and of rare piety.

The officers were very attentive. We were indeed bearers of many recommendations for them from Monsieur de Maurepas.

A third disagreeable feature was the stench and vermin. We had on board a hundred soldiers or so, freshly enrolled, each one of whom carried with him a whole regiment of "Picardie." In less than a week these ravenous

---

Luçon, Apr. 4, 1745,—we learn that he was at Larochelle at that date, and on the point of being named superior of the Seminary.

He returned, consequently, to France in the autumn either of 1743 or 1744. The place and date of his death are unknown.

Of the forty-eight letters which go to make up the *Aulneau Collection* eight were written by Father Nau.

" Picards " migrated in all directions. No one was free
from their attacks, not even the Bishop nor the Captain.
Every time we went on deck, we could see that we were
covered with this vermin. We found them even in our
shoes.

Another centre of infection were eighty smugglers who
had already passed a twelvemonth in durance vile; they
also sent out swarms of marauders. These wretched
beings would have caused the heart of a Turk to melt
with pity.

They were half-naked and covered with sores ; some
even were eaten alive with worms. We clubbed together
and made a collection on board to buy them shirts from
the sailors who had them to spare. All that we could do
did not prevent the outbreak among them of a kind of
pest, which spread throughout the ship, attacking all in-
discriminately, and which carried off twenty of our men
at a stroke.

So those of the officers and passengers who were not
down with it were obliged to work the ship instead of the
sailors. Reverend Father de Lauzon was made boat-
swain's mate for the ecclesiastics.

This sickness afforded a fine field for our zeal. Father
Aulneau distinguished himself by his assiduity in serving
the sick. God preserved him in health during the
passage across, for the good of the ship, but scarcely had
he set foot on shore, when in turn he was stricken down
and brought by two different attacks to death's door.
No one could tell now that he had been sick. I was the
only Jesuit who had nothing to suffer, not even from
seasickness.

We reached Quebec on the 16th of August, that is to
say, the eightieth day from the time of our embarking.
It is one of the longest trips on record from France to
Canada.

What kept us so long at sea was that we always had
contrary winds and so violent that we had to change
our fore-top-mast when off shore near the Grand Banks.
We were eight days tempest-tossed unable to carry a
shred of sail; our ship, like a mere skiff, became the
plaything of the billows, and the seas dashed over the
gunwale as if it had been a shell. A pirate or an English
man-of-war would have made short work with us, had
they attacked us at the time we had so many sick
on board.

We seemed, however, safe from alarms of that kind.
The size of our ship struck fear into all whom we met ;
we frightened even one of the King's vessels we came
across at the Grand Bank. They caught sight of us seven
hours before we noticed them. They immediately bore
away; but the wind was not to their liking, and as we
sailed faster we overhauled them about three in the
afternoon, and relieved them of further apprehension.

Their ship was the Charante, commanded by M. de
la Sauzaie. He sent an officer with "naval refreshments," that is *liqueurs*. We had a good laugh over
their fright; but had they been enemies they would
have had more reason to make fun of us, for they had
the decks cleared for action since eight in the morning,
and we had not a cannon in position to fire.

At last the fatigues and dangers of the sea are past, and
nothing but what is pleasant awaits me. Reverend
Father de Lauzon means to send me to the mission of
Sault St. Louis, where he himself spent seventeen years.
It is the most agreeable and flourishing mission of
Canada. The number of Christian Indians there is
nearly twelve hundred. I will be with Father la Bre-
touniere* and a brother.

* Father Jacques Quintin de la Bretonnière was a native of Meaux, and
born May 5, 1689. He entered the Society Sept. 20, 1710. He arrived in

Father de Gonnor † leaves the Sault, where his services are not of much use, as he has great difficulty in applying himself to the study of the Iroquois language.

Father Aulneau is to pass the winter at Quebec, there to prepare his examination of the fourth year (of theology). He may next spring set out with an expedition to discover the Western Sea, for the Court is absolutely determined to have concerning it more than mere conjecture.

The French who returned this year from the upper country have informed us that the Indians told them that, eleven hundred leagues from Quebec, there are white people wearing beards who are subjects of a king ; that they had horses and other domestic animals. Would they not be Tartars or stragglers from Japan ?

The Indians spoke about the French to these nations, and they were delighted to learn that in Canada there was a white nation bearded like themselves. " The French, to all appearance, are our brothers," they said, " and we would like to see them. Invite them to come here among us."

Canada in 1721 and was appointed to the Iroquois mission of Sault St. Louis, and made his profession of the four vows at that village, Feb. 2, 1726.

In 1728, he acted as chaplain of the Iroquois contingent in M. Marchand de Ligneris' expedition against the Foxes, passing over the present site of the city of Chicago, Aug. 14, 1728. Father Emmanuel Crespel, a Recollet, and a secular priest, François Michel Pellet, attended to the spiritual wants of the remainder of the force.

He acted in the same capacity for a body of 300 Iroquois, forming part of the expedition against the Chickasaws, in the spring of 1739. He died at Quebec, August 1, 1754. *Taorhensere* was the Indian name he bore.

† Father Nicolas de Gonnor belonged to the province of Aquitaine. Born Nov. 19, 1691, he entered the Society Sept. 11, 1710. He came to Canada in 1725. In 1727, he was sent to the Sioux Mission, and afterwards he was stationed some time at Sault St. Louis. In 1749 he had returned to Quebec. thence he was once more sent to the Sault, where he was superior in 1752 There he remained until 1755, when he was transferred to Montreal, and the following year to Quebec, where he died, Dec. 16, 1759. His Indian name was *Sarenhés*.

If this story be true, there is there another grand opening for the Gospel. But we cannot count much on the sincerity of the Canadians (Indians) who have spread this report, for there is no country in the world where more lying is done than in Canada.

The war is still carried on against what remains of the Fox nation, and against the other tribes which have taken them under their protection. Father Guignas* was not taken, as it was feared, but he has had much to suffer, for nothing can be sent him safely. For two consecutive years the provisions sent him have fallen into the enemy's hands.

Father Deblonfort, whom we expected from the province of Lyons, and who had set out from that city for La Rochelle, has not made his appearance in Canada. We do not know what has become of him. It is surmised that Father de Laneurville has enticed him away to the Mission of the Islands.

We stand, however, in much need of laborers : if a dozen came over next year, we would not have too many. I intend to stir them up in the home province by my

---

* Father Michel Guignas was born at Condom in the present *departement* of Gers, France, January 22, 1681. He entered the novitiate of Bordeaux, Dec. 9, 1702. He embarked for Canada in June, 1716. After spending one year at Quebec, he was sent to join Fathers Jean Baptiste Chardon and Joseph Marest, at the Ottawa mission on Lake Michigan. He made his solemn profession of the four vows at St. Ignace, Michilimakinac, on Feb. 2, 1718. Father Guignas accompanied Boucher de La Perrière's expedition to Lake Pepin, where Fort Beauharnois was commenced, May 17, 1727. This was the first post established in Minnesota. The mission bore the name of St. Michael the Archangel. The unsatisfactory issue of the expedition against the Foxes caused it to be abandoned, and while returning with Boucher, the Father was taken by the Kikapous and Maskoutins, August 15, 1728. He was held captive for five months, and was at one time condemned to be burnt at the stake. Dakota and Michilimakinac were the scene of his labors until 1739, when he was transferred to the Saguenay missions in the lower St. Lawrence. From 1740 he resided in the College at Quebec until his death, which occurred on Feb. 6, 1752.

letters, so as to have a good levy. I am writing to some of the willing ones among our Jesuits who formerly spoke to me about their vocation to the foreign missions. I am sure that they will have every facility with your Reve rence in carrying out their design.

I stand as much in need of your fervent prayers as ever, and earnestly ask you for them. I beg you to believe that I will be for life, with the most profound respect,

Reverend Father, your Reverence's most humble and obedient servant,

NAU, of the Society of Jesus.

Quebec, October 20, 1734.

No. 4.

(*Translation.*)

FATHER LUKE FRANCIS NAU TO FATHER BONIN, S. J.

Reverend Father,—Pax Christi—

If I longed to see the "Ruby" safely arrive at Quebec, my longing was scarcely less intense to see her set sail again, that she might bear to you the expression of my kind regards and news from one of whom, I flatter myself, you sometimes think, and who often allows his thoughts to turn with an affectionate remembrance to you.

Here I am at last in a country for a long time the object of my yearnings. Here I am specially singled out to labor for God's greater glory. My happiness must needs remind me that I have to render thanks beyond measure to a God of all goodness for having inspired me with the resolution to cross the seas, but neither can I thank you yourself too much for all your care for me and attention, you the first father, in a spiritual sense, of my soul, since without that special care I never would have had, or at least I never would have followed, that vocation from our Lord.

After God, therefore, it is to you I owe the happiness of having entered the religious state, and of having come to Canada. But what were the dangers I encountered on the way? I give you them here in detail.[*]

Quebec, October 20, 1734.

No. 5.

(*Translation.*)

FATHER AULNEAU TO HIS MOTHER.

(Address:—"A Monsieur Chaterére, Procureur et Notaire Royal à Luçon, pour faire tenir à Madame de la Touche Aulneau,—aux Moutiers—à Luçon—Bas Poitou.)

My Dearest Mother,

I again with joy and eagerness take advantage of the sailing of a vessel for La Rochelle to renew the expression of that respect and affection which I shall bear for you throughout life. I wrote to you already the full account of my voyage on the King's vessel, and you have no doubt received my letter. I hope that it found you in perfect health; my own is now as robust as it ever was. I wrote also, by the same vessel, to my uncle and sisters.

It is now over a month since winter set in here, and at the present writing, the ground is covered with snow. It is as cold as it was in France in 1729. This severity of temperature will increase, and we shall not catch a glimpse of the ground until next May.

This need not alarm your affectionate heart on my account, for we have every means of protecting ourselves against the rigor of the climate and the season. And after all, were it not so, I would not be a subject of com-

---

[*] The particulars which follow are the same as in the preceding letter.

miseration, since I would have more frequent occasion to suffer something for the love of a God who has suffered so much for us./

Persevere, my dear Mother, in beseeching Him to render me worthy by His grace to achieve something for His glory and His service.

Father Nau is on the point of leaving for Montreal or for Sault St. Louis, some seventy or seventy-two leagues from here. I have not yet learned if his appointment be for good. As for myself, I shall start only in the spring ; and I do not know for what place Providence destines me ; but wherever it be I shall find the God of goodness there as everywhere, and I am confident that He will bear me up and not abandon me.

I am writing to Father Faye, who is to make some purchases. In case he is able to execute the commission, be kind enough to send him the money you destine for me. As what I am asking him for is not for myself, the sum will be refunded at Quebec. But if, on the contrary, he should not be able to undertake it, be good enough to send the money to Father Deceron, at La Rochelle, who will make use of it to purchase some books I shall need.

You see, my dear Mother, I do not reject all your loving offers of assistance ; and were they less generous than they are, that would never prevent me from cherishing for you the same sentiments of respect and love. I have often said Mass for you, and I have no greater pleasure than thinking of you. This I do often, and always with feelings of the deepest gratitude.

I am, my dear Mother, with profound respect,
Your most humble and obedient servant and son,
J. P. AULNEAU,
Jesuit Missionary in Canada.
QUEBEC, October 29, 1734.

Please present my respects to my dear uncle and to Mr. Pennot.

No. 6.

FATHER AULNEAU TO FATHER FAYE, AT BORDEAUX.

(There is nothing of special interest in this letter. It is dated from Quebec, Oct. 29, 1734, and bears the following address:—

" Au Révérend Père E. N. S.—Le Révérend Père Faye de la Compagnie de Jésus à la maison professe à Bordeaux.")

No. 7.

(*Translation.*)

FATHER LUKE FRANCIS NAU TO MADAME AULNEAU.

(Address:—A Mademoiselle. Mademoiselle de La Touche Aulneau—Aux Moutiers sur Le Hay.)

Mademoiselle,

Father Aulneau writes to you by the King's vessel homeward bound, and I have the honor of writing to you by a merchantman, so that if news does not reach you by one way you may receive it by another. I have no doubt but that you are very anxious to have some news of a son whom you love so tenderly and with so much reason, so I look upon myself as favored to be able to gratify your wishes in this respect.

I promised to let you know, every year, all that I could learn, comforting or otherwise, about dear Father Aulneau. And to show you with what fidelity and sincerity I intend to acquit myself of my promise, I shall not conceal from you that the health of your dear son was a cause for us of great alarm from the moment we reached Quebec.

Our passage across was one of the longest and most calamitous that was ever made between France and Canada. A contagious sickness broke out on our ship and carried off twenty of our men. Nearly all went through the ordeal.

The great number of sick we had at once to care for afforded but too fine a field for Father Aulneau's zeal to allow of his caring for himself. He set no limit to his charity. He was forever at the bedside of the sick and dying, in the midst of vermin and infection, performing for them the most menial and loathsome services. God preserved his health during the voyage for the consolation of those on board. As soon as he landed he hurried off to visit the sick at the hospital. Fearing that by coming so often in contact with the sick he would himself contract the disease, Reverend Father Superior forbade him positively to set foot in the hospital.

But this prohibition came too late. He had given splendid proofs of his zeal, he must needs now give the same of his patience. He fell sick, and in less than a week he was on the verge of the grave. God, heeding our prayers, restored him ; but our joy was but short-lived, for a few days after he had a relapse which was as dangerous as the first attack, and made us tremble for his life. Thank God, our apprehension is over, and you could not tell now, even, that he had been sick.

He no longer sighs but for the toils of some painful mission. He will, however, pass the winter at Quebec, and will go among the Indians only after Easter.

As for me, who have not been sick, I shall set out at the first opportunity for a mission of twelve hundred Indians sixty-four leagues distant. As my virtue is not so robust, I am assigned to the easiest of all the missions. Father Aulneau, who is of sterner stuff, will not, to all appearances, fare as well. News from him, however, will always reach me wherever he goes, and you may rely on me to keep you informed.

Fear nothing for him, God watches over him. We are in perfect security when we are sustained by so powerful a Master.

It is becoming bitingly cold, and I can scarcely hold my pen.

I recommend myself earnestly to your prayers, and I am with profound respect,

Mademoiselle, my very dear Mother,*

Your most humble and obedient servant,

F. NAU,

Of the Society of Jesus.

QUEBEC, October 29, 1734.

I present¦my respects to Monsieur Paynot, and I beg him to remember me at the Holy Sacrifice.

No. 8.

FATHER H. FAYE, TO MADAME AULNEAU.

(A short note transmitting a letter from F. Nau to Reverend Father Provincial, dated Bordeaux, Jan. 11, 1735, and bearing the following address:—

A Madame—Madame la Veuve Aulneau—Aux Mou-tiers—Recommandé à M. le Directeur de la poste de Luçon—à Luçon, Bas Poitou.)

---

* He thus addresses her as she was the mother of a brother in religion.

No. 9.

(*Translation.*)

Extract from a letter of : —

FATHER AULNEAU TO FATHER H. FAYE.

QUEBEC, April 25, 1735.

Reverend Father,—

The Peace of our Lord Jesus Christ—

I am happy to take advantage of the last moments I am to pass at Quebec to send you one more token of my respect and attachment, and to thank you beforehand for all the letters, news and whatever else I asked you to send me over from France. I suppose that my mother sent you the 100 francs, and that you were able, without putting yourself out too much, to make the purchase I had taken the liberty to trouble you with in my second letter. Should you not have been able to do so, I am not the less sensible of your kindness.

I am about to add twelve hundred leagues to the distance which already separates us. Reverend Father De Lauzon sends me off to discover other Indians whom not one of us has yet set eyes on, of whom we have heard only through the " Assiniboels " and " Cristinaux," and who dwell three hundred leagues beyond the two latter nations.

It will be among the last mentioned, however, that I shall pass the winter, nine hundred leagues from Quebec, as it will be impossible before then to push further into the heart of the country.

To the tribe which is to be the ultimate object of my mission, they have given the name of " Ouant Chipouanes "—that is, *those who dwell in holes;* until now, they have remained unknown to the rest of men. Thus, if our good God so wills it, and preserves my life, I shall be the first to bear to them the tidings of the Gospel.

You can easily imagine that I shall not be in a position to undertake with any hope of success, at the outset, their instruction. I must first set about learning their language, and I have nothing which can be of any assistance to me in that study. It will only be by dint of frequent converse with them that I shall, with our Lords' help, manage little by little to compile grammars which may be of use to the missionaries who will come after me.

I have been commissioned to do the same for the language of the *Cristinaux* and *Assiniboels*, among whom the French have been but a short time, and who have scarcely ever heard mention made of Jesus Christ, for they have come in contact with but a few of the French, and these few have picked up here and there but a word or so of their language.

I am directed not to remain permanently with these tribes, because they rove about and have no fixed dwelling place. On the contrary, the *Ouant Chipouanes,* if what is said of them be true, have permanent establishments, and consequently there is a better promise of doing good among them.

Such, Reverend Father, is the undertaking confided to my care. It is certainly beyond my strength and would call for a degree of virtue far higher than what I possess ; for there I will be for at least three or four years without the least spiritual succor, and removed several hundred leagues from any other priest. You will not find it difficult to comprehend that it is the severest trial I could meet with in life. I confess that I can only look upon my destination with fear and trembling for my eternity.

What reassures me is that it is not through any choice of mine that I find myself thus exposed to so many dangers. I even did what I could to have another missionary appointed to accompany me. I succeeded to the extent of having one promised me, if they send one over from France, and some are expected this year.

⎛Seven or eight of our missions had lately to be suppressed for want of evangelical laborers, and there are others where there is but one missionary, and one is not enough to work with fruit. When an occasion presents itself, plead hard, Reverend Father, in behalf of our missions, for though missionaries here do not find as much comfort and consolation as in many other countries, these are not wholly wanting, while they will find here more numerous occasions than elsewhere of suffering and of becoming more like their model, Jesus Christ crucified.⎞

So true is this, Reverend Father, that the most of those of whom Providence makes use for the conversion of the poor savages are men in whom we see reproduced all that virtue and saintliness which the Society admires in the most holy of her children. I have met with them nearly all this winter, and the striking example they have given me of zeal, recollectedness, self-denial and interior union with God has, through our Lord's mercy, awakened in my heart a true and sincere desire to make every effort I can to imitate them.

Would that it were possible for me to make known to you all that has edified me in the lives of some of them, for I am sure you would be moved even to tears. I know one among others to whom I opened my heart and who honored me also with his confidence. I had occasion to admire all that I had heard and read of in the lives of the most eminent in sanctity in the Society.

We lost during the winter Father Guênier, of the Pro-

viuce of France. We still deplore his loss, and if the sanctity of his life did not inspire us with the utmost confidence that he is now engaged praying for us in heaven,
we should give a freer vent to our tears.

He was a man of unwearied zeal and of great mortification and prayer. He had a most tender devotion to the
Blessed Virgin, and it might be said that it was in some
sort his very.devotedness to the Mother of God which
was the cause of his death. Worn out with fatigue and
labors, persuasion was used to induce him to take some
rest and to intrust to another the duty of preaching on
the feast of the Assumption of Our Lady. But he gave
for reason of his persisting desire to preach that he
believed that it would be the last sermon of his life, and
that he would be happy before dying to give once more
some further proof to the Blessed Virgin of his devotion
and love.

I had the happiness of listening to him, two days after
we landed, and it was one of the best delivered, beautiful
and impressive sermons that I ever heard. It was indeed
the last he preached, and during the short time he
passed on earth after it, he set us the example of every
kind of virtue.

It was my privilege to watch at his bedside for two
nights during his last illness, and consequently to be
witness of the admirable sentiments to which he gave expression. They were such, Reverend Father, that we read
of in the lives of Saint Aloysius and Saint Stanislaus.

The whole country round mourned for him as for an
apostle. During au entire day that he lay exposed after
death, there was no one who did not come to bedew the
coffin with his tears, or to beg him to be an intercessor
in his behalf before God. Had a watch not been set, his
clothes would have been cut up for relics. As it was, and
in spite of every precaution, this could not altogether be

prevented, and he was shorn of nearly all his hair. We were obliged, willingly or not, to take everything he had ever made use of and distribute it among the people.

Pray God, Reverend Father, to grant me a death as precious in His sight as we have reason to believe was that of this saintly religious. I shall be exposed to many perils ; raise your hands sometimes to Heaven to obtain for me all necessary grace to undergo the hardships which Providence may hold in reserve for me for my sanctification.

I remain, Reverend Father, with profound respect and in union with you at the Holy Sacrifice,

Your very humble and very obedient servant,

J. P. AULNEAU,

of the Society of Jesus.

OBITUARY OF FATHER FRANÇOIS BERTIN GUESNIER, BY FATHER PIERRE DE LAUZON.

The following circular or obituary letter, written by the Superior of the Canada Mission, and sent to the houses of the Order in France, does not belong to the Aulneau Letters which we here interrupt to make place for it.

It is the translation of a copy made some years ago at the request of the late Father Félix Martin, from the autograph original preserved in the archives of the Gesù in Rome.

The striking confirmation of the correctness of the main features of Father Guesnier's life and character, drawn from the preceding letter of Father Aulneau, is sufficient to convince us that though more enthusiastic in his pane· gyric of the virtuous religious, Father de Lauzon is not to be taxed with exaggeration.

As this document has never been published, and as it may serve to supplement Letter No. 9 of the Aulneau Collection, it naturally finds its place here.

The only other item of interest we have been able to discover, relating to Father Guesnier, and not mentioned either in the obituary or in Father Aulneau's letter, is that, when asking Reverend Father General to send him on the foreign missions, Father Guesnier's first pious impulse was, provided his superiors should grant his request, to take part in the re-establishment of the missions in Japan.*

(Translation.)

QUEBEC, October, 1735.

REVEREND FATHER, — P.C.—

The Mission of Canada could not have met with a greater loss than the one it sustained last year by the death of the late Father François Bertin Guesnier, who departed this life December 18th, 1734, at this college, aged about forty years. He died of a disease of the chest and throat, accompanied by frequent hemorrhage of the lungs. This disease he contracted, while yet in France, by a too close application to study, and by the efforts of his ardent zeal for the salvation of souls.

God, who can work out His designs without our co-operation, called him to Himself at a time when he appeared to be more indispensable to the country, and just as he was beginning to disclose more manifestly the rich treasures of nature and grace with which he was gifted for the perfect discharge of the duties of his state.

He was blessed with a keen intellect and a retentive

---

* De Guilhermy, *Menologe*.

memory, and by assiduous endeavors to master all he thought that he was in duty bound to know, he had greatly widened the range of his acquired science. He was naturally eloquent, and though in conversation he was averse to trifling, he so charmed his interlocutors that his company was sought for by all who wished to improve.

But his virtue was even of a higher order than his ability. It was after a retreat he made at the close of his first year of teaching, that he drew up a plan of life more inward than he had hitherto led. From that period he adopted for maxim, that a member of his Order should never be satisfied with an ordinary degree of virtue, nor ever leave any good undone in whatever he had undertaken for his own or for his neighbor's sanctification.

Hence that precision in the fulfillment.of his every duty, which constituted him at home a living rule and a true apostle abroad. Hence also, that continual recollectedness which always prepossessed others in his favor ; that unceasing watchfulness over himself ; that spirit of faith with which he was ever animated, living in the presence of his Saviour, whom he never lost sight of even in the midst of occupations the most distracting. Hence his devotion to Our Lord and His Holy Mother, with which he strove to inspire all whom he directed ; his piety in the recitation of his office and in his other devotions, which he always performed kneeling in the most respectful posture. To these he every day, at the foot of the altar, added other long prayers which the rigor of the climate could never force him to interrupt.

His fasts were of daily occurrence, and he seldom touched wine. Sometimes he tempered his other austerities, when so directed by obedience, but he resumed them when he was left free to do so, through a desire to observe his rule, which he knew bade him deny himself unceasingly and seek in all things his greater mortification.

It was not through vanity nor to make a display of a learning which inflates, that he indefatigably applied himself to study, but through a sense of duty, and because he was thoroughly convinced, as he was wont to say, that a member of the Order without science would be like a soldier without arms, incapable of glorifying God in the exercise of his vocation.

Our colleges in France, where he resided a greater length of time, and that of Quebec, which Heaven was content to bless with barely a glimpse of him, can testify that such was his character, and that, as the letters from Europe which announced his coming declared, one would have to go far to find a Jesuit at once more holy, more learned and more painstaking than Father Guesnier.

Scarcely had he landed than it became evident why he had asked with so much earnestness to cross the seas, volunteering for the most arduous missions. He would have gone to the Esquimaux, who are reputed to be a species of cannibal, never yet rendered tractable, and this with the idea, that the sooner he should be devoured the sooner would he consummate his sacrifice.

But obedience—for he was its submissive child—appointed him to a class of theology. Any other than Father Guesnier, whose constitution was frail, and whose health was already badly shattered, would have found this occupation sufficient. But this eager missionary, who had a greater dread of sparing himself than of shortening his days, and who had not bid farewell to France, where he had toiled hard already, to adopt a life of ease in a foreign country, undertook whatever other good work came within his reach.

He preached the word of God from time to time, and he did so with such soundness of doctrine, energy and unction that he was listened to with delight.

The Men's Sodality, which is very numerous and flour-

ishing at Quebec, was intrusted to him. It would be hard
to conceive a care greater than that he expended on it, or
a fervor more intense than that which he revived among
its members.

Without mentioning the work of the confessional in the
church—and his, owing to the confidence he inspired, was
seldom empty—he took upon himself the spiritual direction of our boarders, who will ever hold him in grateful
remembrance for the sound principles he inculcated. With
this, he catechised what we call the little school, made up
of more than a hundred children who are learning to read
and write. It was a pleasing task for him to cast into
their tender hearts the seed of Christian piety.

A man of great versatility of genius, able and willing
to undertake anything, he gave himself over without
reserve to these varied occupations, which were, he
claimed, the indemnification due him for the Esquimaux
mission he had not been able to obtain

And what clearly shows the extent of his ability, and his
great courage, and how God sustained him, he performed
each separate duty with as much thoroughness as if he
had no other task to accomplish. He exchanged the
class room for the pulpit, the pulpit for the confessional,
and the confessional for the bedside of the sick, edifying
all by his modesty, his sweetness of temper, his endurance
and his charity.

If there was in his conduct one thing more than another
which excited admiration, it was that, ever busy, and so to
speak, actively employed night and day, he never made
mention of his occupations nor of himself. To blame
others was as distasteful to him as was self-praise. It
would be impossible to convey an idea either of the abundant blessings which so virtuous a demeanor drew down
upon the work of this worthy laborer, or of the pious
emotions which were awakened in every heart by his holy
example.

As it is no exaggeration to say that few apostolic men are to be found so dead to self, so intent on saving souls, so eager and so successful in the work of promoting God's glory, so might I add, that seldom elsewhere is so great concern manifested for the safety of apostolic laborers as in this colony, which always showed itself deeply interested in his preservation.

On his arrival, at the very point of leaving the ship, he was temporarily incapacitated for work by a hemorrhage from an old lesion in his chest. The citizens betrayed their apprehension of losing him by tokens of anxiety, evidently the most sincere. Not only our own and all the other religious communities, but seculars, men and women, joined in novenas to obtain his recovery. The degree of earnestness, though intense, with which they besought Heaven not to take from amongst them a man of such uncommon merit and virtue, was not greater than the degree of Father Guesnier's own indifference and resignation to whatever Our Lord should ordain concerning him.

We were graciously heard ; but later an affection of the throat, which complicated his lung disorder, and which in spite of every remedy, became incurable, reduced him to a state of extreme languor ; but he always bore with heroic courage the sharp pains and prolonged weariness inseparable from so grievous a complaint.

As he drew nearer day by day to the term, he exerted himself to bear his ills with twofold patience and love of God. For the three months he was confined to the infirmary, he spent his time in repeated reviews of his faults, expressions of regret for his past shortcomings, fervent confessions and communions, devout aspirations and ardent longings to be united with God.

More than a month before his death, he besought those who visited him to speak to him of God only. All else had no relish for him. To his last breath, he exhibited the same contempt for life, the same strength of soul and the same trust in his Saviour.

He was asked one day if he had no scruple at having worn himself out with his vigils and labors. He answered as did St. Aloysius, that he was more apprehensive lest he should not have done enough for God. When he was given up by the physicians, the most distinguished persons in the city came to recommend themselves and their children to his prayers, believing, without the least misgiving, that one whose preaching and exemplary life had drawn them nearer to God during his earthly career could not but have great influence with God after death.

He died a week after having received the last sacraments. He employed these last days in continually uniting his own dispositions with those of our Saviour during His agony and while on the cross. The morning of his demise he had the office of the dead recited for him, and he passed to a better life tenderly kissing the crucifix and with his dying lips pressed to the wound of the Sacred Heart of Jesus, for which he had a particular devotion.

He had scarcely breathed his last, when people of every rank in the city gave proof of the lofty idea they entertained of his virtue, and of a sense of the great loss they had sustained. This loss was declared to be a universal bereavement, affecting the whole colony, which now found itself deprived by death of Father Guesnier, an incomparable laborer, who, in the short space of twenty months, had achieved as much for the salvation of souls as many others in as many years.

The exclamation, " He was a saint," was on every lip, and constituted, as it were, his funeral eulogy. Each vied with the other to secure some object which had belonged to him. People flocked in from the outlying districts of Quebec to his obsequies, at which all the citizens were present. So that from time out of mind, our church, where already many celebrated Jesuits were interred, was never so full to overflowing as on the day of his burial.

Nine months has he been buried, and yet not a day has passed but some one of his spiritual children has come to pray on his grave and to commend themselves to him.

I shall not, however, the less solicit of your Reverence the ordinary suffrages for this our beloved departed, who-after having laid deep the foundation of his sublime perfection in Old France, crossed over to this New France to put the crowning to the structure, having striven so closely to live here the life of St. Francis Regis, whom he had chosen for his model. Deign also to grant a share in your Holy Sacrifices at the altar to him who has the honor of being

Your Reverence's

Most humble and obedient servant, ·

DE LAUZON, Jesuit.

No. 10.

(Translation.)

FATHER AULNEAU TO HIS MOTHER.

(Address :—Monsieur Cbaterere, Procureur et Notaire Royal à Luçon, pour faire tenir à Madame de la Touche Aulneau, aux Moutiers sur le Hay—à Luçon.)

My dearest and most honored Mother,

I continue to observe faithfully the promise I made you, and it is with the greatest pleasure that I once more offer you a token of my most sincere and most respectful attachment. I passed the winter at Quebec in the enjoyment of perfect health, and indeed very pleasantly. I am now on the point of departure, and thenceforth I must devote my thoughts to the work of saving the Indian.

My joy would be complete had I been able to secure the companionship in my expedition of another Jesuit. But Providence has not seen fit to grant me that consolation. God alone from this out must be my only consolation. Beseech Him to grant me the grace of never rendering myself unworthy by my sins of His protection and of the effects of His mercy.

The objective point of my mission is too remote to admit of the possibility of my reaching it this summer. I shall be obliged to pass the winter nine hundred leagues west of here at a post occupied by a few Frenchmen, on the shores of a great lake. It will be from that place that I shall write you next spring. As it might very well happen that my letters will not have reached Quebec before the departure of the ships for France, do not be alarmed, my dear mother, if you receive no news from me. I shall beg Father Nau, who is stationed at an Iroquois mission sixty-four leagues from Quebec, to write to you every year, and to make up for what it will be impossible for me to do myself as often as I would wish.

The Indians, among whom I am to be sent, have remained until now unknown to the rest of the world, and have never seen either a Frenchman or a missionary ; so, if it be God's good pleasure, I shall be the first to announce Jesus Christ to them.

I shall have to travel twelve hundred leagues before reaching them. They are said to be very humane. It is said also that they receive kindly those who visit them, that they have horses, cattle and domestic fowls, so you see, my dear mother, that I shall not be very much to be pitied while among them.

I shall not be able to labor very effectually] in the beginning at their conversion, not being acquainted with their language ; at the outset the most I shall be able to do will be to baptize children at the point of death, and

thus send them to Heaven to pray for the conversion of
their parents, and for the one who, by conferring on them
baptism, thus will have procured their happiness. You
may be sure that I shall keep you fully informed of
any success with which the good God may deign to
bless my labors.

Were I not so much pressed for time, I should write to
my dear uncle, to Melle. de la Sicaudière and to Madame
de la Villedieu ; but I have not now leisure to do so.
Be kind enough, my dear mother, to make up as much
as possible for the deficiency, and convey to them the
expression of my kind regards. Although very far from
them, I do not nor shall I ever forget them. If I do not
write to my brothers, it is for the same reason ; I beg you,
however, when you see them to greet them affectionately
for me. I recommend myself to their prayers.

As for what you may think fit to send me, please
forward it to Mr. Dupan, merchant, St. Yon street, La
Rochelle, addressed to brother Boispineau, the elder,
Quebec, to send on to Father Aulneau, missionary at
Fort St. Charles on the Lake of the Woods, Canada.

Lastly, my dear mother, redouble your prayers for me.
It very seldom happens that a day goes by without my
recommending you to God at the Holy Sacrifice of the
Mass ; so that I hope that our Lord, touched by the
prayers which we offer up one for the other in our
separation here on earth, will unite us for ever in the
abode of His glory ; then will we congratulate ourselves
for all eternity for having made some sacrifices for so
great a Master. Let us love Him always, and love Him
alone, for He alone deserves our love. Let us serve Him
with ardor, and make every effort to render ourselves
like unto His adorable Son dying on the cross, for there
is the model of all Christians and more especially of
missionaries. Wherefore in our trials we have no other

more certain reliance nor other more powerful motive to brace ourselves up to suffer them with joy and resignation. Happy the one who is deemed worthy to die for Him.

I am, my dear mother, with the most profound respect and the most tender affection,

Your most humble and most obedient servant and son,

J. P. AULNEAU, J., Miss.

Many assurances of my respectful consideration to Mr. Pennat. I recommend myself to his Holy Sacrifices.

QUEBEC, April 29, 1735.

No. 11.

(*Translation.*)

Extract from a letter of

FATHER AULNEAU TO FATHER BONIN.

REVEREND FATHER,—

The Peace of our Lord Jesus Christ—

The lively interest you always took in what concerned me while I was in France encourages me to think that you will be glad to learn what my destination is, now that I am so far from you. It may be that it will make you tremble as much as I do for my salvation. If anything gives me confidence it is that I have had no hand in it myself. Reverend Father de Lauzon, my superior, has singled me out for the mission, to which he sends me without consulting me, in spite of my natural repugnance. God's holy will be praised ; for He alone will now be my consolation, and whatever help I count upon will be derived from Jesus expiring on the cross.

I am here about to set out on a journey of twelve hundred leagues, to go among savages who have never yet

met a Frenchman nor a missionary. I cannot reach
their country this summer ; I shall be obliged to pass the
coming winter nine hundred leagues from here, part of
the time with the Christinaux and part of the time with
the wandering tribes of the Assiniboels, who, in their
expeditions, so they tell us, have met these Indians
whom I am to seek out. They call them in their language
Ouant Chipouanes, which means dwellers in holes.*

Doubtless in all this travelling about I shall have to
undergo many hardships ; they would have been more
than welcome had it been advisable to give me as companion another Jesuit, but I am to be sent alone
among these tribes, whose language as well as whose
manner of living are unknown. I humbly confess,
Reverend Father, that it was not without a pang that I
brought myself to obey. May God accept the sacrifice I
make of my life and of all human consolations for the
expiation of my sins. My hope is that He will not
abandon me, while I find in the consideration of Jesus
Christ crucified enough to strengthen me to bear with
all the hardships, and to overcome all the difficulties
which Providence may have in store for me.

I shall be removed several hundred leagues from any
other priest, and in that lies the greatest hardship of all

---

* In Father Francis M. Picolo's report to the Royal Council of
Guadalaxara, concerning the then recently established missions in California, and dated February 10, 1702, we find the following passage :

The country is thickly peopled in the interior, and especially in its
northern parts ; and although there is scarcely to be found a village which
does not consist of twenty, thirty, forty or fifty families, they have no
houses. The shade of the trees protects them from the heat of the sun
during the day, and they construct a kind of shelter of branches and
foliage as a protection against rainfalls at night. In winter, they shut
themselves up in caves which they excavate in the earth, and there they
live crowded together not unlike animals.

Bethune edition of the *Lettres Edifiantes*, 32mo, Paris, 1830, Vol. 13, p.
197.

my mission, because I am far from flattering myself that I shall seldom need to cleanse my soul in the blood of Jesus Christ. But God seems to require of me the sacrifice of this very consolation. I can refuse Him nothing ; let His Holy Name be forever blessed.

To reach my final destination I shall have to cross nearly the whole of North America ; but my course is so ordered, that instead of passing by the Mississippi River, when I have got as far as Missilinakinac, where Father Saint Pé is stationed, I shall take a northwest direction, and shall traverse all the great lakes which lie on this side and beyond the sources of the Mississippi, until I come to the lake of the Assiniboels. I shall leave that post only in the spring, to journey on three or four hundred leagues beyond, in quest of the Ouant Chipouanes, so that my course then will be southwest.

Such, Reverend Father, is the route I shall follow towards an objective point which you see is very indefinite and uncertain, since all we know about it is founded on the reports of other Indians, who, for the most part, have little scruple in speaking differently from what they think.

If what they add concerning the place where the Ouant Chipouanes dwell be true, I should say that these cannot be very far from California, for, if we are to believe their reports, the Ouant Chipouanes dwell on the shores of a great river where there is an ebb and flow in the stream, which would go to show that the sea cannot be very far off. It is not easy to determine what river this is. I am led to surmise, however, that it is no other than the great river which Father King, a German Jesuit, mentions in the map which he traced of the regions lying to the north of California, and which he calls the Rio Colorado de Norte. See the fifth collection of the *Lettres Edifiantes**

---

* I have not been able to find this map of California in the *Lettres Edifiantes.*

4

Whatever be the truth relative to these conjectures and to the place where these Indians dwell, I am deputed to go in quest of them, and to establish a mission among them if it be possible. All this, Reverend Father, is much beyond my strength, wherefore I have placed myself and whatever betides my enterprise in the hands of our Lord. Beg Him to prepare me for every eventuality according to His holy and divine will. Do not forget, either, to send me some nourishment for my soul; nothing could please me more than what you might suggest, by way of encouragement, to animate me to serve and love Him who alone deserves our service and our love.

Father Nau is permanently stationed at the Iroquois mission of Sault St. Louis, near Montreal. We are much afraid that Father Guignas has been taken and burnt by a tribe of Indians called the Foxes; but in this unfortunate country we should set little value on our own lives which are so often in peril. I should deem myself happy were I judged worthy of laying mine down for the One from whom I received it. I recommend myself to your Holy Sacrifices, in union with which I am, Reverend Father,

Your very humble and very obedient servant,

AULNEAU, Jesuit missionary.

QUEBEC, April 29, 1735.

No. 12.

(Translation.)

FATHER AULNEAU TO HIS MOTHER.

(Address:—A Monsieur Chaterere, Procureur et Notaire Royal à Luçon, pour faire tenir à Madame de la Touche Aulneau, aux Moutiers sur le Lay—à Luçon.)

MY DEAREST MOTHER,

The long stay which I have been obliged to make at Montreal, quite contrary to my expectation, affords me an opportunity of sending you the renewed assurance of my respectful attachment. I start to-morrow, without, thank God, any other sorrow than that of going too far away to be able to write or to receive letters from you as often as I would wish. Perhaps three hundred and forty leagues from here I shall find leisure to write to you again ; if so, I shall take advantage of the opportunity with the greatest pleasure.

You see the career that Providence has opened out before me ; pray God, my dear Mother, that I may acquit myself in a manner worthy of Him. I trust, that, separated for His sıke from all that might afford human consolation, He will not forsake me ; and that if in the midst of the forests, whither I go to pass the rest of my life, and in the midst of wild beasts I find nothing to flatter my self-love, I may find at least an opportunity to destroy and annihilate it by my sufferings. Conjure our Lord to send me many sufferings and to give me patience to bear them with resignation conformably to His holy and divine will.

Nearly every day I pray for you at the Holy Sacrifice of the Mass, and shall continue until death to offer this one only mark which lies in my power of the gratitude I owe you.

I remain, my dear mother, your most humble and obedient servant and son,

J. P. AULNEAU,

Ind. Miss. of the Soc. of Jesus.

MONTREAL, June 12th, 1735.

I beg you to present my respects to my dear uncle, Mr. Pennot, and Madame de la Villedieu. I embrace and send my love to my brothers and sister. My dear mother-please remit to Father Bonin, the Procurator, the allowance you have been kind enough to make in my favor.

No. 13.

(Translation.)

FATHER AULNEAU TO HIS SISTER THERESA,
Religious of the Union Chrètienne of Fontenay.

MY DEAR SISTER, the peace of our Lord Jesus Christ.

Quite contrary to your expectation and my own, you receive this one more letter from me. I know that it will be anything but a cause of annoyance to you, otherwise your friendship for me must have greatly changed. I leave Montreal to-morrow, where my stay has been longer than I was led to expect. I count upon reaching the first term of my mission towards the end of the month of November. To all appearances it will only be after many hardships. I shall be happy, my dearest of sisters, if I draw that profit from them which God has a right to expect. He should never appear to us more worthy of our love, nor seem to love us more, than when He gives us the opportunity of becoming more like unto His own beloved Son, every phase of whose mortal career was marked by some new suffering.

It will be three or four years, as I wrote you in my last letter, before I shall have any fixed or permanent abode, and am not likely to do much else than wander about from forest to lake in view of acquiring some knowledge of the country to which Providence sends me. If I had more virtue than I possess I would congratulate myself much more on being obliged to commence thus to devote myself to missionary life as so many other holy missionaries had begun, who in the early times of French settlements in this desolate country watered the wilderness with their sweat and with their blood; but my lack of virtue fills me with apprehension.

Pray, therefore, more and more for me, and beseech the ladies of your community to do the same. Assure them also of my deep gratitude and respect.

If you can, without drawing upon what is given you for your own needs, procure for me some altar linen and decorations, you would afford me much pleasure. I am in this respect in a pitiable condition of penury. Good-bye, my dear sister, and let your love for me in our Lord Jesus Christ be as deep as mine is for you.

J. P. AULNEAU, Jes., Ind. Miss.

MONTREAL, June 12th, 1735.

No. 14.

(*Translation.*)

FATHER AULNEAU TO FATHER FAYE.

REVEREND FATHER, P. C.—

I thought that the letter which I wrote to you from Quebec would be the last I could send you this year, but my unexpectedly long stay in Montreal procures me the pleasure of writing to you once more before striking into the forest wilds.

Since Father Nau took up his abode at the Sault St. Louis mission he has suffered from a violent attack of the gout, and this has been the cause of general regret among the missionaries of this needy country. As for myself, with every increase of active work my health has become more robust, and the closer insight I have of the worry and sufferings of the life I am to lead, the more thankful I am that God has deigned to call me to the missions of this forlorn country.

I wrote you 'previously that I was about to penetrate into a region hitherto unknown, in view of making Jesus

Christ known to savages who have never even heard Him spoken of, and who in turn have never been seen by us. All this foreshadows many hardships, the least of which will be that I shall have to wander about in the woods four or five years with no fixed habitation. In this, though very different as to merit and virtue, I shall resemble the first missionaries of this poor country who watered it with their sweat and blood.

Implore our Lord to grant me the grace of walking in the footsteps of so many holy and great men.

Since my last letter we have received news from Father Guignas, who since 1732, when we last heard from him, has undergone so heroically all that hunger, thirst and persistent threats of being massacred and burnt by the Sakis or Foxes could inspire of horror. He is fairly worn out, but the dearth we are in of mission· aries precludes the possibility of relieving or succoring him. Beg God to send us help. Those who come over to devote themselves to our missions will yet find here the most admirable models of every virtue.

I remain, Reverend Father, with the most profound respect and in union with your Holy Sacrifices,

Your most humble and most obedient servant,

J. P. AULNEAU, Jes., Ind. Miss.

MONTREAL, June 12th, 1735.

Do not be surprised if you do not hear from me for two or three years. I shall be too far away to be able to give you any news sooner. Should you write to me, be kind enough to address your letters to Father Aulneau, S.J., Missionary at Fort St. Charles on the Lake of the Woods, Canada.

No. 15.

(Translation.)

FATHER AULNEAU TO FATHER BONIN.

Reverend Father, the peace of our Lord Jesus Christ.

I eagerly take advantage of the remaining moments I have to spend in Montreal to write you a second, and perhaps the last, time in my life. I leave to-morrow for the woods. In a former letter I told you what was to be the object of my mission; allow me, Reverend Father, to recommend it again to your Holy Sacrifices. As for the missionary, I am convinced you will not be unmindful of him at the altar.

We received, a few days ago, news of Father Guignas; since 1732 he had not been heard from. He is in a help·less state. The hunger he has had to endure, the imminent danger of being massacred by the Sakis and the Foxes to which he has been continually exposed, and numberless other hardships, borne heroically, have brought him so low, that even the Indians, who have little pity for us, are forced to look upon him with feelings of compassion. We are, however, in the impossibility of attempting anything for his relief, owing to the scarcity of missionaries. Pray God, Reverend Father, to send laborers to this needy mission. Another cause of anxiety for us is that Father Nau was laid up last spring with a violent attack of the gout.

I beg you to send me the reckonings of the eclipses of sun and moon visible in France and America. I shall endeavor to turn them to account, to the best of my ability, in determining the longitudes of the new regions to which Providence is sending me. I shall communicate whatever observations I may think likely to be received

by you with satisfac!ion. For that matter, I cannot ex·
pect to receive before three or four years what I now
take the liberty of asking you, owing to the great
distance which separates us.

I remain, Reverend Father, with the m?st profound
respect, and in union with your Holy Sacrifices,

Your most humble and most obedient servant,

J. P. AULNEAU, Jes., Ind. Miss.

MONTREAL, June 12th, 1735.

No. 16.

(*Translation.*)

FATHER NAU TO FATHER BONIN.

(State of the Iroquois Mission of Sault St. Louis in 1735.)

Reverend Father, the peace of our Lord Jesus Christ.

I question much whether the letter I had the honor
of writing you last year gave you more pleasure than
yours afforded me. Several ships had already arrived
from France, and had brought letters to nearly all our
missionaries, and not one brought a single word to my
address, though my post is one of the nearest to Quebec.
Imagine my joy when a letter was handed me from the
one of all persons in the world whom I esteem most, and
to whom I am most deeply indebted! The good opinion
you entertain of me covers me with confusion and
strengthens my endeavors to become all that you fondly
suppose me to be already, and, in fact, that I should be.
I feel the need of being spurred on in the accomplishment of my duties. Though I am here surrounded by
holy missionaries, and have continually before my eyes
perfect models of virtue, I am still full of defects.

This year, I am in a position to speak to you of Canada with more certainty than last year. The climate is salubrious, the quality of the soil excellent, but the natives are indolent. The winter is not so severe as we are told in France. We never experience more than three or four days in succession of extreme cold. The thaws have been of such frequent occurrence this year that the drawing of fire-wood was accomplished with difficulty. More precautions against the cold are taken here than in France. We are warmly clad, and our apartments are heated with stoves. All in all, I suffered every year more from cold in France than in Canada. My health is of the best, were it not for a violent attack of gout I suffered after Easter*, and which laid me up for a month and a half. Even now I have a twinge every day, but that does not prevent me from going about, nor was it the cold that brought it on. I had already felt its approach while yet in France.

To speak correctly, we have but two seasons here,—winter and summer. In this mission the winter is shorter by a full month than at Quebec. We are in fact forty leagues more towards the South. Sault St. Louis † is not to be found marked on the maps; this is not sur-prising, as it is only since these maps were made that our mission has grown into an important village. Our latitude is 45 degrees and 30 minutes, and we are distant three leagues and a half from the town of Montreal, which lies to the North-east, on the other bank of the river.

It is imagined in France that the Iroquois, who formerly treated with so much cruelty the French whom they made captives in war, must be of ferocious aspect, and that their very sight and name would strike terror into

---

* Easter fell in 1735 on the 10th of April.

† Sault St. Louis is better known at present as Caughnawaga.

all who encounter them. This is pure fancy. Generally
speaking, you could find nowhere finer looking men.
They are of better build than the French, while side by
side with the Iroquois other Indians seemed dwarfed.
Nearly all the braves of our mission are nearer six feet
in height than five. Their countenance is in keeping
with their stature, and their features are regular. The
children especially are diminutive types of the picturesque
(*sont des miniatures*), transparency of color being alone
wanting. Their complexion is of an olive tint, but not
so tawny as that of other tribes, not differing much from
that of the Portuguese. I have met even in the streets of
Bordeaux any number of men darker than our Iroquois.
They would for the most part be as clear-complexioned
as the French, were it not for the effects of the smoke in
their wigwams, which is so dense that I fail to understand
how they do not lose their sight.

The costume of the Iroquois is different from that of
other Indian tribes. Their hair is trimmed somewhat
like that of the Recollect Fathers, with this difference,
that they raise in a bunch the hair of the crown by means
of a kind of wax mixed with vermilion, and allow a few
hairs to protrude above, to which they fasten a porcelain
bead or so, or a feather of some bird seldom met with.
Over the shirt they usually wear a garment of French
fashion, with lace sewed on all the seams. When the
weather is cold, or on gala days, they wear a cloth
mantle a yard and a half square, the lower border of
which is trimmed with eight or nine bands of lace.
Their *milasse*, that is their leggings, are adorned with
ribbons and a variety of flowers broidered with elk-
hair dyed red or yellow. These are made to fit closely,
the better to show off the elaborate finish of the work
Their moccasins are of smoke-dried deer-skin. Some
wear silk stockings and shoes of French make and silver

buckles. Among the Indian nations all the women are dressed alike. You have no doubt seen the likeness of the Indian maiden, Catherine Tegab-kouita, who died in odor of sanctity ; all the squaws are similarly dressed.

As for the question of morality, the Iroquois and Hurons are more inclined to the practice of virtue than other nations; they are the only Indians capable of refined feelings; all the others are to be set down as cowardly, ungrateful and voluptuous. If there were no French in Canada we would have as many saints in our mission as we now have Christians ; but the bad example and solicitations of the whites are a very great bar to the sanctification of our Iroquois. Though it be forbidden under the severest penalties to give fire-water to the Indians, and though, during the last two months, exemplary punishment has been meted out to four Frenchmen, one of whom was condemned to imprisonment, two to be whipped by the public executioner, and the other to be fastened by the neck in the pillory for having carried on this illicit trade, still our Indians find all the fire-water they want, and as soon as they are drunk they are capable of any crime.

Not three months ago, an Aigonquin, in a drinking-bout, killed with three stabs of a knife a poor soldier who was quietly working in a house at Montreal. Arrested on the spot, the Indian thought he would escape punishment because he was drunk and did not know what he was doing. He was condemned notwithstanding to be hanged ; but as the executioner was away he was killed by a blow on the head.

Should any one of our Indians make his appearance in the village while in a state of intoxication, he is obliged to submit to a public penance. He is to remain kneeling outside the church during Mass and the other prayers made in common, for ten or twelve days, according to the gravity of the scandal given.

Drunkenness is the great vice of the Indian ; but, thank God, we have many who never touch intoxicating liquor of any kind. Those who do drink do not do so often, and, taking all into consideration, our Iroquois are much better Christians than the French.

Before giving you an account of the exercises of our mission, I must tell you, Reverend Father, how I was adopted into the Iroquois nation. It is a necessary formality, for a missionary would not be an acceptable person in the village were he not a member of the tribe.

Two months after my arrival, I invited the elders to a banquet. The spread consisted of a whole carcass of beef, bread in proportion, two bushels of peas and a quantity of tobacco. When all were assembled, Reverend Father de Lauzon, who had lived many years in this mission, made a long speech for me. Three Iroquois orators answered in turn. When the speech making was over, one of the elders rose and announced that a name must be given to the back robe, for this is the appellation by which the Jesuit missionaries are known. After having gone over all the names of former missionaries, he determined that I should hereafter be called Hatériata, and I now go by no other name in the village. Ask God in your prayers to give me the grace of realizing to the fullest extent its signification, for Hatériata in Iroquois means "The Brave," the magnanimous man.

It now remained to assign me to a lodge, and to adopt me into a family. I had the honor of being enrolled in the Family of the Bear. You must know that in the village there are three families : that of the Bear, that of the Wolf and that of the Tortoise. All new comers are made members of one of these three families. The family of the Tortoise has become so numerous that it has been divided in the Big and Little Tortoise.

And now let me say something about the exercises of

the mission. At day-break, be it in winter or summer, Father de la Bretonnière says the first mass, at which all those assist who have to go out to the fields to work. They recite their morning prayers, and then the beads, in two choirs. An hour later, I say the every-day mass for the whole village, during which the prayers and hymns of the Church in keeping with the season are sung in two choirs also. After the mass, I gather the children together in the church and make them recite their morning prayers, and then teach the boys how to serve mass.

About nine o'clock, Father de La Bretonnière puts the adults who have not yet been baptised through their catechism. The remainder of the day is spent going about visiting the sick and in deciding disputes which may have arisen in the lodges. An hour before sunset, I assemble the children again in the church for their evening prayers and for the recitation of their catechism. As soon as the children are dismissed the men and women repair to the church for the recitation of their prayers in common.

On Sundays and festivals I am in the confessional until ten in the morning, when I sing high mass, after which I preach to the French, for I have charge of a French parish, and there is no other church than that of the mission.

Other members of our French population, who flock from all sides to the tomb of the servant of God, Catherine Tegahkouita, to accomplish the vows made in time of sickness, keep me pretty busy.

At one in the afternoon, Father de la Bretonnière assembles in turn the Indians who are members of the Sodality of the Blessed Virgin and those who belong to the congregation of the Holy Family, to give them a short exhortation. We have, as you see, in the village two associations,—the Sodality and the Holy Family. To be qualified to become a member of the Holy Family, one must have passed through the Sodality and have given unmistakable proofs of fervor, for its members are all really devout souls and, to say the least, are as worthy members as are those in France. Several practise austerities which many a religious would hesitate to undergo.

At four in the afternoon Vespers are sung, after which Benediction of the Blessed Sacrament is always given. There could be nothing more decorous than the behavior of our Indians while in church and during their other devotional exercises; the very sight inspires devotion. Father Aulneau, who happened to be here on the feast of Corpus Christi,* could not restrain his tears of joy and devotion while the procession lasted. All our braves were in their war accoutrements with the exception of the bearers of the canopy and the chanters. The squaws and children followed in symmetrical order, most pleasing to the beholder. Three shrines had been prepared at intervals where the Blessed Sacrament was set down, and at each halt a volley of musketry was fired and five mortars exploded.

For our Indians, singing is a necessary adjunct, as they are incapable of prolonged mental application, and it is on this account that all their prayers are set to music; really, it would be a great pity were it not so, they suc. ceed so admirably. I often wished that Reverend Father Landreau, who is so fond of well executed church music, could be present at our grand masses, it would be a greater treat for him than anything he has yet listened to. The braves who lead off with the first verses he might take for a choir of a hundred Cordeliers, and the squaws for some great community of nuns. But what am I saying?

---

* June 9, 1735.

Neither Cordeliers nor nuns ever sang as do our Iroquois
men and women. Their voices are both mellow and son-
orous, and their ear so correct that they do not miss a
half-tone in all the church hymns which they know by
heart.

Our Iroquois, like all the other Indian tribes, with the
exception of the Sioux, are sedentary. They raise horses,
pigs, poultry and other domestic animals as do our own
people. The braves leave us about the end of September,
each taking his own road to the hunting grounds of the
deer and beaver, nor do they return to the village before
the month of February. Others go on the war path. We
have actually forty warriors out on expeditions to strike
at other tribes. Their weapons are ever ready, for they
take the part of the French in every quarrel with the
other Indian nations,—indeed, the Iroquois of Sault St.
Louis are looked upon as the most warlike of all the
American tribes; but this is no proof of their valor.
Their mode of warfare is but stratagem and surprise, their
encounters are mere attempts at assassination. They
fight bravely then only when they know that the sole
alternative lies between victory or death.

Our people have a war on their hands this long time
with an Indian tribe called the Foxes. It has been in a
very slight degree successful, through the impossibility in
which our troops are of ever overtaking them in sufficient
numbers to destroy them. Last year, ninety of our young
braves joined the French expedition against the Foxes,
but after inconceivable hardship and a journey of more
than seven hundred leagues,* their guides led them astray,
and they were obliged to make their way back without
having caught sight of the enemy save in one in-

* The distance to the Fox country and back would be about seven
hundred leagues.

stance. A party of twenty-three Indians, nearly all of
our Mission, and seven Frenchmen had somehow
become separated from the main body when they found
themselves suddenly surrounded by a war-party of two
hundred Foxes. Our warriors would have been wiped
out had it not been for the resolution of the Iroquois
captain. "We are all dead men," he said, "if we surren-
der. There is no help for it; we have to sell our lives as
dear as we can. Let us show these Foxes that we are
Iroquois and Frenchmen." Whereupon he led his braves
to the attack. The enemy could not withstand the first
onslaught, but retreated precipitately to their fort.
Thirty Foxes were laid low and ten taken prisoners; our
party lost but two Frenchmen and one Indian.

The majority of the adults whom we instruct for
baptism in the village are slaves taken in war. I had
the consolation of administering this sacrament to two,
and Father de La Bretonnière to four, since I am stationed
in the Mission, that is about a year ago; there are a
dozen or so yet remaining who will receive Baptism at
Christmas. It thus happens that it is our warriors who
contribute most to the increase of the Mission.

The five Iroquois nations, who are with the English,
are visibly on the decrease, on account of their incessant
quarrels and the use of intoxicants supplied by the
English. It is for this reason that the more provident
abandon a country where they cannot live peaceably, and
come to settle among us.

Others who are accused of witchcraft are also obliged to
take refuge at Sault St. Louis, otherwise they would be
put out of the way at the first opportunity. A family of
Mohawk Iroquois have come but lately to settle in our
village. It is thus that the devil himself unwillingly
becomes the occasion of the salvation of these wretched
fugitives by making it less difficult for them to embrace
Christianity.

The instruction of the slaves is our hardest task, for
they seldom learn the language well, and it is very hard
to make them understand what we would have them
know. We have had here in the Mission for the last ten
years an Indian woman of the Fox nation, and she does
not know how to speak Iroquois yet.

Iroquois and Huron are the only two difficult languages; we must, however, be familiar with them both in
our Mission, because all the prayers are in Huron. These
two languages have a common origin, but differ from
each other as much as French and Spanish. All our
Indians understand Huron and prefer it to Iroquois,
though the pronunciation is not so pleasing to the ear.
Hence it is that they do not care to recite their prayers in
their own native tongue.

I told you that I taught the children their catechism,
manuscript in hand of course, for after ten months of
study I cannot be very proficient in Iroquois. I am
beginning nevertheless to understand and to make myself
understood, but I would not dare yet to speak in public.

You expressed the wish, Reverend Father, that I
should give you all the information possible concerning
the Jesuits of our province who are now missionaries in
Canada. I shall not be long.

Reverend Father de Lauzon, superior general of the
Mission, is universally esteemed, and with reason. He
did his best with Reverend Father General to be allowed
to resign his office, which is a real burden to him for
more reasons than one, but it was decided that he should
complete the ordinary term of six years. So we shall
not have him back in our Mission before their expiration.

Father Chardon has been stationed for the last two
years at the residence in Montreal ; he is looked upon as
one of the most holy Jesuits sent out to Canada. Father
Guignas is in the Sioux country, at a little French fort

with but six men with him. Scarcely a month ago the Marquis of Beauharnois, governor general of New France, sent twenty-two men in four canoes with supplies of which he stood absolutely in need, for the Sioux refuse to provide for him. It is not at all certain that the relief party will reach him without molestation, their route lying close to the country of the Foxes.

Father De Saint-Pé, who has for companion Father Du Jaunay, an old fellow-student of mine at Nantes, will return next year from Missilimakinac, to take charge of the Men's Sodality at Montreal.

Father de la Richardie spent the winter at Quebec, where he did a world of good by the two general retreats he preached. The mention of this Father's name reminds me that I must take back what I wrote you last year when as yet I was not well informed of what concerns the Hurons. I said that there were no other Christian Hurons than those of Loretto. In fact, seven years ago there were no others; but Father de La Richardie found means to gather together at Detroit the dispersed Hurons, all of whom he converted. The mission numbers six hundred Christians.

Le Detroit,* at the forty-second degree of latitude, is situated between Lake Huron and Lake Erie. This stretch of country is the finest in Canada; there is scarcely any winter, and all kinds of fruit grow there as well as they do in France. There is question of building a town there. Seventy French families are already on the spot, and there is a fort and garrison of which the Reverend Recollet Fathers are chaplains.

Father De Gounor is at the mission of Lorette, but he is subject to frequent attacks of sickness.

Father Aulneau, as robust as he is courageous, has set out for the Western Sea ; he will arrive there only next summer. The first missionary who lands from France

---

* Le Detroit, *i.e.,* the Strait, was the name given to the shores on both sides of the river.

will go to keep him company, otherwise he would not be able to remain there long alone, as he will be four hundred leagues distant from Father Guignas, who is his nearest neighbor.

I had a pretty long conversation with Mr. La Verandrie, who is in command of the three most western forts · I understood from the interview that not much reliance can be placed on what he says concerning white, bearded Indians. The Western Sea would have been discovered long ago if people had wished it. Mons. le Comte de Maurepas is right when he says that the officials in Canada are not looking for the Western Sea but for the sea of the beaver.

It is to be hoped that Father Aulneau will find more docile Indians than the Ottawas and the Sioux, among whom Fathers Saint-Pé and Guignas are laboring with little success. They have managed to convert but a few old men and women who are beyond the age of sinning. The greatest good they can effect is to baptize children when they think they are on the point of death ; those that recover seldom fail later to fall away from the faith.

Let me know on what particular points you desire information concerning Canada and our mission more especially, and I shall endeavor to satisfy your pious curiosity.

Not a day goes by without my begging our Lord to shower down His choicest graces on the one who was instrumental in procuring for me the greatest of blessings, —in having me received into the Society of Jesus. Pray for me in turn unceasingly, and for my mission.

I have the honor to remain with the most profound respect in union with your Holy Sacrifices,

Reverend Father,

Your most humble and obedient servant,

L. F. NAU, of the Society of Jesus.

SAULT ST. LOUIS, October 2, 1735.

No. 17.

(Translation.)

FATHER LUKE FRANCIS NAU TO MADAM AULNEAU.

(Address:—A Mademoiselle.—Mademoiselle de La Touche Aulneau, aux Moutiers sur Le Lay.)

Madam,

I am far from blaming the sentiments with which nature inspires you with regard to your dear son, Reverend Father Aulneau, for they are quite proper and reasonable. The greater the merits of Father Aulneau the more sensibly you should be affected at being separated for ever from so amiable a son. You are right in grieving for him as if he were dead for you, but your sorrow is a Christian sorrow, and there is no danger that your maternal tenderness should go to any excess. Were there any danger of that kind, the Christian spirit which animates you would soon bring it within bounds.

Nothing could be more heroic than the fresh sacrifice which dear Father Aulneau has just made in setting out for the Western Sea. But, after all, it is his very vocation which imposes similar sacrifices, and so noble an enterprise was worthy of his great heart. It was, moreover, obedience which bade him undertake it. I find at least as much greatness of soul in your submission to the orders of Divine Providence as was required in Father Aulneau's case. It must have cost you many a pang thus to surmount the promptings of nature, and to sacrifice the feelings of maternal love to the glory of our Lord; but the greater the pain the more meritorious will your generosity be in the sight of God.

I had dear Father Aulneau here with me for two weeks; I saw him perhaps for the last time; he was then full of strength and health, and was longing for the conversion of the Indians of the Western Sea. He set out three

weeks after Pentecost for his destination, which is eleven
or twelve hundred leagues distant, where no Frenchman
has ever set foot, and which he will reach next year only.
I candidly confess that on that occasion my courage was
not as great as yours. It was with tears I embraced him
before he left the mission-house, and I went and hid myself so as not to witness his departure.

Since then I received a letter from him, dated July 27,
at the mission of Missilimakinac, three hundred leagues
from here. He rested there eight days, and then set out
for a French fort, seven hundred leagues from this place.
I conjecture that he must be very near the end of his
travels for this year. At the melting of the snows he will
resume his journey. I dare say it is the longest, most
painful and dangerous one ever undertaken by a missionary in Canada.

He will not suffer from want of food such as it is; it
consists of flour to be formed into paste, and Indian corn
of which *sagamité* is made; but he has with him an
attendant, who is an excellent huntsman and who will
supply him occasionally with game. He has a pretty
good escort, but should the unknown tribes he is in quest
of harbor any evil designs against him, what could twenty
Frenchmen do against a whole nation? You see, my
dear mother, that I have little consideration for your
maternal feelings, but you insisted upon my being
outspoken. Next year I shall receive other letters from
Father Aulneau, and perhaps he will enable me to impart
more welcome news than I have done this year.

As for myself, I am stationed in the most flourishing
mission of Canada, where I am in want of nothing. My
health, however, was a little shaken by an attack of the
gout this last spring; I have not got quite over it yet.
But we must suffer something for God, and were it not
for this infirmity I should have for my share nothing
but the sweets of life.

The three letters you did me the honor to write me reached me safely, the two first coming by the same vessel. Recommend me often to our Lord, my very dear mother. Every day I pray Him to strengthen your courage and resignation to His holy will. I have the honor to remain with the most profound respect, Madam,

Your most humble and obedient servant,

L. NAU, of the Society of Jesus.

SAULT ST. LOUIS, October 3, 1735.

I pray you, present my excuses to Madam Aulneau, the religious *De la Foy*, at Fontenay. The bearer of these letters to Quebec is in too great a hurry to allow me time to write to her. If she could send me next year a little package of beads and other articles of devotion, I should be exceedingly obliged to her, and would try to forward a part of them to Father Aulneau.

No. 18.

(Translation.)

FATHER JEAN P. AULNEAU TO FATHER BONIN.

Fort St. Charles, among the Kristinaux, April 30, 1736.

REVEREND FATHER,—P.C.

The letters I had the honor to write to you last year, 1735, caused you, no doubt, some surprise. I therein took the liberty of asking you for certain things which my lack of experience in the missions, whither Providence has called me, and I know not what fancy, alone could have suggested, nor should I be at all surprised if you paid no attention to those requests. Let me ask you to pardon me for all the trouble and bother I may have caused you. The erratic life I must needs lead would prevent me from totiug about anything but what is strictly indispensable. Moreover, the money which was to be advanced would have scarcely sufficed to buy a quarter of all I asked your Reverence. Once more, Reverend Father, pardon me my want of discretion.

I reached Fort St. Charles October 23rd, 1735. I had set out from the Iroquois mission of Sault St. Louis June 21st, the feast of St. Aloysius, under whose protection I believe Providence intended that I should place myself, in thus foreordaining that the day of my departure and of my complete separation from all that could afford me any satisfaction should, contrary to all appearances, be delayed until the festival of that great Saint. With the assistance of so powerful a protector I enjoyed perfect health to the end of my journey.

There are, counting from..............° hundred leagues, nearly all by water and canoe............ I stopped with Father de Saint Pé at Missilimakina...... I went back fifteen leagues on the distance already covered so as to take the route by Lake Superior. We coasted along the Lake for the space of two............ following, as is customary, the north, sometimes the west and southwest..........of Lake Superior. We struck inland into the regiou which lies to the north of Lake....and after having journeyed nearly always on foot for the space of two or three days, we headed some· times towards the west, sometimes towards the southwest and sometimes eveu towards the south, threading our way among a profusion of lakes. Several of these lakes have a circumference of more than a huudred leagues.

From the upper extremity of Lake Superior to Fort St. Charles, whence I have the honor of writing to you, the distance is set dowu at three hundred leagues. We

---

* There are several passages in the original manuscript torn off or defaced by time.

journeyed nearly all the way through fire and a thick
stifling smoke, which prevented us even once from
catching a glimpse of the sun. It was the Indians who
in hunting had set fire to the woods, without imagining,
however, that it would result in such a terrible conflagra-
tion.

So long a journey through any other country would
have been diversified by a number of interesting features
calculated to awaken one's curiosity, but all that was to
be met with in this vast region was limited to lakes, rocks,
immense forests, Indians and a few wild animals. So that,
Reverend Father, I can communicate nothing to you
deserving of attention. On one occasion, however, while
on the shores of a large lake which the French call the
Lake of the Cross (Lac de la Croix), and which is about
one hundred and twenty leagues from here, I thought I
saw a lunar eclipse; it was on the 1st of October,—if it
were truly an eclipse and not merely an effect of the
smoke. It ended about nine o'clock at night. I noticed
also, on several occasions, especially while on Lake
Huron, grand displays of the aurora borealis; but in-
capacity, more even than lassitude, did not admit of my
taking observations with sufficient accuracy to give you
an adequate idea of them. We have witnessed here
throughout the winter the same phenomenon, and
scarcely a night has passed but the northern skies have
been all aglow with the aurora borealis.

And what, Reverend Father, of Fort St. Charles, where
I have passed the winter? It is merely an enclosure made
with four rows of posts, from twelve to fifteen feet in
height, in the form of an oblong square, within which
are a few rough cabins constructed of logs and clay and
covered with bark.

It is about a league in the.............. from sixty

to seventy leagues, on the southwest side of the Lake of the Woods.*

This lake is..........leagues in circumference. Its greatest length is north.........Several streams put it in communication with other lakes, all of which empty into another which the Indians say is larger than .... They call it Ouinipigon. This latter, further on, gives rise to three........rivers which empty into the sea, as well as I can conjecture from what the Kristinaux say, beyond Port Nelson.

It is on the shores of this last lake, about one hundred and fifty leagues from here, that I purpose passing a part of the summer with the Assiniboels, who occupy all the land to the south of it. The lands on the remaining sides are taken up by the Kristinaux, who occupy not only all the northern part as far as the sea, but all the immense stretch of country beginning at the Lake of the Woods and extending far beyond Lake Ouinipigon also belongs to them.

Some time about the feast of All Saints, if it be the will of our good Lord, I purpose, with as many of the French as are willing to encounter the same dangers, to join the Assiniboels, who start every year, just as soon as the streams are frozen over, for the country of the Kaotiouak or Autelssipouncs to procure their supply of corn. It is to evangelize these tribes that my superiors send me here. From Lake Ouinipigon to their country the distance is computed to be two hundred and fifty leagues, but as the party engage in the hunt as they advance, in all likelihood we shall go over more than four hundred. If

* The probable site of Fort St. Charles was a few miles up the bay now known as "North West Angle Inlet." At the entrance of this bay, which begins at American Point, lies Bucketé Island. The latitude of the fort would be about 49° 6´ and its longitude west of Greenwich 95° 4´, or perhaps a few minutes further west. The words of the original manuscript which are defaced or torn off might be supplied (by italics) thus : " Il est environ à une lieue dans la *profondeur d'une baie distante du lac La Pluie* de 60 ou 70 lieues, au sorouest du lac des Bois."

we manage to reach there in season, I shall not be satisfied
with visiting the first villages of the Kaotiouak, but shall
push as far on as I can along the shores of the river
where they dwell and where the Kristinaux say they
have seen sea-wolves. This would be a sure sign that
they are not very far from the sea.

Towards the middle of March I shall leave this place
to return to the shores of Ouiuipigon. I omitted to tell
vou, Reverend Father, that Fort St. Charles, according
to Monsieur de la Jesmeraye, ensign of the detachment
of the marine quartered in this country, is situated at 48°
5'. This is all the information, Reverend Father, I am
able to give you at present concerning this wretched
country. It may be that I have not expressed myself
correctly, but you will pardon me I am sure. In any
case, I do not vouch for the truth of all I have told
you, and which I have not learnt from personal observa-
tion but from the report of the Indians and a few Frenchmen, whose experience is but slightly more extensive
than my own. At some future date, perhaps, I shall be
in a position to give you something more reliable on this
vast extent of territory so little known. If I have risked
speaking to you at all about these wilds, it was merely to
gratify you.

As for the Indians who dwell here, I do not believe,
unless it be by miracle, that they can ever be persuaded
to embrace the faith ; for even not taking into account
the fact that they have no fixed abode, and that they
wander about the forests in isolated bands, they are su-
perstitious and morally degraded to a degree beyond conception. What is most deplorable is that the devil makes
use of the very men who should endeavor to break their
bondage to rivet their fetters more firmly. Both English
and French, by their accursed avarice, have given them
a taste for brandy, and have thus been instrumental in

adding to their other vices that of drunkenness, so that brandy is their only topic of conversation, the sole object of their petitions, nor can they ever be counted upon unless they receive enough to get drunk on.

The good God has already chastised more than one of our fellow-countrymen engaged in this infamous traffic by visiting them with financial ruin ; but neither the loss of temporal goods nor the fear of the loss of God in eternity has as yet availed to abolish so shameful a trade.

This, Reverend Father, constitutes one of the greatest crosses which the missionaries have to endure here ; it has brought about the destruction of several flourishing missions, and has induced many an Indian to cast aside every semblance of religion. There were a certain number of Mousouis, neighbors of the Kristinaux, and not a few other Indians among those who dwell in the vicinity of the western extremity of Lake Superior, who had received Holy Baptism, and who have been replunged through drunkenness into their former superstitions.

I must, however, say in justice to the French with whom I have journeyed, that they have not mingled in this infamous traffic, and that in spite of all the reiterated demands of the Indians they have preferred to ignore all offers of barter from the tribes than give them brandy in exchange.

Notwithstanding the shameful vices of these poor infidels, God has allowed them still to retain certain notions which, perhaps, might help to determine them to range themselves on the side of religion. They acknowledge the immortality of the soul. After its separation from the body it goes to join those of the other deceased Indians ; but these have not all the same dwelling-place—some inhabit enchanting prairies, where all kinds of animals are to be found. These they have no trouble in slaying, and with the viands of the chase they are perpetually regaling each other. No wonder if everywhere, on these plains, you see kettles swung over the fire, and dances and games,—all told, that is their paradise.

But before reaching it, there is a spot of extreme peril, —the souls have to cross a wide ditch. On one side of the way, it is full of muddy water offensive to the smell and covered with scum, while on the other the pit is filled with fire which rises in fierce tongues of flame. The only means of crossing it is on a pine tree, the ends of which rest on either bank. Its bark is ever freshly moistened and besmeared with a substance which makes it as slippery as ice. If the souls who wish to cross to the enchanting plains have the misfortune to fall at this dangerous passage, there is no help left; they are doomed for ever to drink of the foul, stagnant water, or to burn in the flames, according to the side on which they fall. Such is their hell, and such is their obscure notion of what efforts must be made to secure heaven.

I leave untold a thousand other vagaries, of which, from the little said, you may form a faint idea, nor am I sufficiently versed in the matter, having but a very imperfect knowledge of their language. If it be pleasing to you, I may revert to the subject later on.

I am the first missionary who has as yet undertaken to systematize the language of the Kristinaux. All ...... I am not very skillful at it. I have picked up but little during the winter, as all have been out on a warlike expedition against the Maskoutépoels or Prairie Sioux. They destroyed a few lodges, and some have returned with a few scalps, which are prized as the most precious trophies of their victories. This war was the occasion for us of much suffering during the winter, as we had no other nourishment than tainted pike, boiled or dried over the fire.

The Kristinaux are not near so numerous as the Assini-boels, but they are much braver, or rather much more

fierce and cruel. They massacre each other on the most
trivial pretext. The war and the hunt are their sole
occupation. They are averse to teaching their language
to others, so that what little I know has been picked up
in spite of them. I hope, nevertheless, before my departure for the Koatiouaks to announce the Gospel to them.

The devil is the only idol they acknowledge, and it is
to him that they offer their outlandish sacrifices. Some
have assured me that he has visibly appeared to them
They are in great dread of him, as, according to their own
avowal, he is the author of nothing but the ills which be-
fall them. It is for this reason they honor him, while
they do not give a thought to God, since He sends them
nothing but blessings. They acknowledge having received everything from Him, and that He is the author
of all things. Wherefore they manifest no surprise when
told of His wondrous works. Even the raising of the
dead to life would not astonish them. One day, a Mousouis, listening to the story of Lazarus, exclaimed:
"Wonderful indeed, that God raised him to life! He had
already given life to him once, could He not give it to
him a second time?"

When we speak of Christianity to them, one of their
standing reasons for not embracing it is, that the Indians
were not made for that religion; but the true reason,
which they do not wish to avow, is their fear of the devil,
and the necessity in which they would be placed of
renouncing what they call their .... which they imagine
they could never abandon without immediately being
stricken with death.

Beg our Lord, Reverend Father, to enlighten these poor
bondsmen of hell, and to touch their hearts. Conjure
Him especially to send into these vast regions zealous
laborers, to announce the Gospel to them, and to oblige
them, with Heaven's help, to cherish and embrace a reli-

gion that they cannot help respecting. I am convinced that if there were five or six missionaries in this region, their efforts would not be fruitless, especially among the Assiniboels and the Koatiouaks, who are much more tractable than the others. But what can one poor mortal do in such an extent of country, the very limits of which are as yet unknown ?

Scarcely have we fairly entered upon the question of religion with some one of the natives, and commenced to entertain some faint hope of his conversion, than, confronted with the necessity of supplying the wants of life, he has to betake himself to an erratic life in the woods. There the devil invents a thousand subterfuges to turn him from his purpose, and makes him ashamed that he ever lent an ear to what was said to him about the other world.

Were there several missionaries here, it would be otherwise. They would be stationed at different points, and could head off, as it were, the roving savage, who, if he escaped from one, would fall into the hands of another. But independently of this, I am altogether too weak and too unworthy to inaugurate a work which would require a missionary of consummate holiness. I submitted this to my superiors before my departure, but my representations were not deemed of any weight.

A promise, however, was made to send me a companion this year; if one comes, I hope through the mercy of God that in a few years I shall be able to give you news which will be satisfactory.

Before the new missionary can reach me here, I think that I shall have acquired a pretty complete knowledge of the language of the Kristinaux and a smattering of that of the Assiniboels, for Providence has endowed me with a certain facility in mastering these odd *jargons*.

After all, what the issue of all these projects will be is

known to God alone, and, who cant ell, perhaps instead of receiving the announcement of their realization you may hear the news of my death.

The journey yet before me is one of......leagues, even should I not chance to meet with any barbarous treat·ment or incur the fierce resentment of the savages of the countries through which I have to pass. I place all in God's hands. I am disposed to offer Him with a light heart the sacrifice of my life. It is already too long that I continue to offend Him, so it will never be too soon for Him to chastise me.

I beseech you, Reverend Father, and in spirit I cast myself at your feet to conjure you to remember me in your Holy Sacrifices, me, the most unworthy of creatures. It is in union with these sacrifices that I remain,

Your Reverence's most humble and obedient servant,

J. P. AULNEAU, Jesuit Missionary.

I would beg you, Reverend Father, to convey the ex-pression of my respect to Reverend Father Superior and to all our Fathers. I recommend myself to their Holy Sacrifices also. As the last canoes are on the point of leaving, I shall not for a long time have another oppor-tunity of writing. I reluctantly close this letter, im·portuned as I am to finish by those who are to carry it. Please to recommend me often to our Lord at the Holy Sacrifice of the Mass, and be assured that no one can be more respectfully attached to your Reverence than yours,

J. P. A.

No. 19.

(Translation.)

FATHER BESSOU TO MADAME AULNEAU.

(Address :—A Madame—Madame La Touche Aulneau, Veuve—Aux Moutiers sur Le Lay—en Bas Poitou—par Luçon).

LA ROCHELLE, Feb. 18, 1736.

Madame,

I received yesterday evening, at half-past eight, the letter you did me the honor to write to me. The one who handed it to me told me that he had it already for some time, but that he had forgotten to deliver it. His thoughtlessness was very near depriving me of the pleasure of receiving it, for had the winds been as favorable as they were last Sunday, we should have sailed Monday morning at five. I congratulate myself that through the postponement of our departure I am now in possession of your missive. Had it been otherwise, you would have accused me of negligence for not answering, and with reason, though I should not have been in the wrong, as no letter had reached me.

I feel grateful to dear Father Aulneau for having thought of me and having mentioned me in his letter to you ; but I am still more grateful for the letter you took the trouble to write, to wish me a prosperous voyage.

I should have liked very much to have started for Canada. I had asked for this mission in a particular way from Father General ; I had explained to him that I felt better able to stand the cold there than a hot climate ; he had promised me in the answer he wrote that he would bear in mind my preference, but he has disposed of me

otherwise, the urgent needs of the Cayenne mission having caused him to modify his first resolve. God's will
must be accepted ; but I confess, all the same, that I
was not a little surprised at the change. I had but a
confused idea of the nature of the Cayenne mission,
for I imagined that the climate was excessively hot,
and for that reason quite incompatible with my
temperament, and in acquiescing I offered the sacrifice of
my life to our Lord. It is to be hoped that He accepted
it as a grateful offering. Since my departure from Poitiers, I have heard from persons who have sojourned in
the country that the heat there is not so intense as one
might naturally conjecture, from the fact that it lies so
near the Equator. This advantage, however, can in nowise
compensate for the pleasure I should have experienced in
seeing once more our dear Father Aulneau, for I had
promised to join him, as he very likely told you before
his departure from France. He was well aware of my
leaning to the foreign missions. From the time that we
lived together at La Rochelle, friendship had united us ;
Providence now severs us. The great distance which is
to separate us will not lessen that friendship, at least I so
flatter myself. I had not the virtue necessary for a mission where there is as much to suffer as there is in the
field of his labors. I might have proved an impediment
to the good he is to accomplish in that barbarous region.
I trust that the fruits garnered will be abundant : his
ardent zeal, his eminent virtue and his love of suffering
make me count on it.

You should congratulate yourself on having a son worthy of you, who will be the first to announce the mystery
of the cross to nations who have never heard of it. The
character of the tribes for whose conversion he is to labor
leads us to believe that his efforts will not be in vain.
They are less barbarous than the other Indians of

Canada. They will consequently be more inclined to turn to profit the useful lessons he will impart to them of a God dying for their salvation. These Ouantchipouaues have herds of cattle and horses to cultivate the land, which shows that they are not such wanderers as are the other natives.

The Indians amongst whom I am to labor are not less erratic than those of Canada. Hunting and fishing are their only occupations. They always carry a knife in their hand as a Frenchman would carry a cane. They are mild of disposition provided you do them no wrong, or at least provided they fancy you intend none ; but to convert them permanently they must be brought to adopt more sedentary habits. Their wanderings will be a great drawback to their instruction.

My Mission will not be on the islands but on the main land, somewhere in the vicinity of the Amazon River, a thousand leagues or thereabouts from Canada. If God preserves my life and health, I do not despair some day of seeing Father Aulneau. We cannot tell what may happen. Some of our Fathers who are in Cayenne came there from Canada, and perhaps there will be some who will leave Cayenne for Canada. If I never again have the happiness in this world of embracing my dear friend, I hope to meet him in heaven. Opportunities for sancti-fying myself will not be wanting : I have but to profit by them. I shall not have as much to suffer from cold, it is true, but I shall have to bear with other discomforts which will be equivalent to it. Beg God that I may know how to use them with advantage, and that I become a fitting instrument to work for my own salvation and that of others.

Since you look upon missionaries as your fathers, brothers and sons, deign to number me among the latter. If to deserve this privilege it be sufficient to cherish a true attachment for yourself and the rest of your family, I think my title is as valid as that of any other, I had the honor of two or three interviews with you at Luçon ; I met your daughter at Fontenay, and have heard our Fathers speak of her in eulogistic terms : I was intimately acquainted with your three sons, and appreciate their many good qualities, and it would be impossible for me not to hold them in high esteem and to bear for them a sincere attachment. Though I have not seen Michael since he was my pupil, I have heard that he remains always steadfast in the performance of his duty, and that he gives you every reason to be satisfied with him by faithfully seconding the care you take in the matter of his education. When you write to him, pray assure him of the kind remembrance of him I still entertain. I fully appreciate the trouble he took to come to Luçon in hopes of seeing me. It would have been an unfeigned pleasure for me to have met him ; I indeed counted on going there but obedience called me elsewhere.

Do not forget me when you write to Canada. I should have written myself to Father Aulneau, but that I feared my letter would miscarry. I may even do so yet if our voyage is postponed for any considerable time. Though we are waiting only for favorable winds, the weather does not seem disposed to smile upon us.

I shall not fail to write you not only after my arrival in Cayenne but every year and oftener, if I find a means of sending my letters. You will confer on me a great favor and a great honor by sending me news of yourself and family. I recommend myself to your prayers, and be persuaded I shall not forget you in mine.

I have the honor to be with all possible esteem and respect, Madam,

Your most humble and obedient servant,

BESSOU, Jesuit.

No. 20.

(Translation).

FATHER BESSOU TO MADAME AULNEAU.

Kourou, May 18, 1736.

MADAM,—

I am keeping the promise I made you when I answered the most obliging letter you did me the honor to write to me at La Rochelle. I can give you little else than the particulars of my sea-voyage, which was prosperous. I suffered from seasickness in going from La Rochelle to the ship, but once on board I experienced no further trouble. God was very bountiful in preserving my health in spite of the rough weather which lasted nearly a month. The winds were so unfavorable that we were borne at one time towards the coasts of Ireland, at another towards those of Portugal, and again further south towards those of Africa. We had most to suffer off Cape Finisterre, for after having beaten about in the teeth of the gale for eight days, our officers thought themselves lucky to find that they were about in the same place. Our position, however, was far from being enviable, for we were near the Cape, and the winds and waves were driving us towards the breakers. Night and day the officers were on deck, and the Captain had already decided to bear away and seek shelter in a Spanish port, when God was kind enough to send us a more favorable wind, just what was needed to extricate us from our perilous position. We were fifty-four days at sea.

I shall remain but a few days in Cayenne, and am at present at Kourou with Father Lombard, who has already passed twenty-seven years with the Indians. He has gathered around him about six hundred natives, all lead·

ing a most edifying life. They are a fickle people, and
that is why the missionaries endeavor to bring them together, the better to watch and instruct them, and especially to ground them more and more firmly in their
religion.

This zealous missionary has had much to suffer, and
was obliged to make *men* of this tribe before attempting
to make *Christians* of them. Formerly they had no religion, and it is a very arduous task to impose the
restraints of Christianity on a people who have never
borne the burden of any law. They are very tenacious of
their freedom; to attempt to curtail it would spoil all.
It was for this reason that the King forbade the French
to settle among them or to molest them.

There are in these parts four distinct nations, the most
numerous of which are the Galibes. They enjoy the
reputation of being the most polished of the country, but
their refinement is very primitive, and to which full justice is done when we say that they are a trifle less
barbarous than the neighboring tribes. The whites have
heard of the existence of thirty different peoples; there
are others far inland yet undiscovered, so the Indians
themselves tell us. It is for us missionaries to go in
quest of them. I am confident that we shall manage it,
provided we receive more help, and that God sustains us
with His grace.

I am to leave here after the feast of Corpus Christi* to
go among the Pirious, for such is my destination. I
must first learn their language before undertaking the
work of their conversion. It appears that they are
well disposed, and have asked for missionaries as some
other nations have also done; but we have not missionaries enough to satisfy all who ask.

---

* In 1736 Corpus Christi fell on the 31st of May.

It is a hard life, for, the missionary has to live in the wild woods, this whole vast extent of country being but forest land. The woods are the abode of serpents and wild beasts of formidable size. Bread is unknown to the country whither I am to go, and there is no possibility of carrying flour on the journey, on account of the rapids and falls. We must ascend the River Oyapok in canoes hollowed out of the trunks of trees; and were they not made exceedingly light they could never be carried up round the rapids. So you see that if we consider merely the country, I have not lost much in not going to join our dear Father Aulneau. It is here that my Canada will be. The natives with whom I shall have to deal will be less ferocious, it is true, but I shall be far from a friend dearly loved, and who, I flatter myself, prizes my friendship in return. God thus willed it, and may His Holy will be done.

It will be a happiness for me to make known Jesus Christ to nations who have never heard of Him. I shall labor to this end as long as God blesses me with health and strength. Pray that He may make me strong, and that He may grant me all the graces necessary to work for the sanctification of these poor Indians and for my own.

When you write to Father Aulneau, do not fail to assure him of my esteem and of the friendship I cherish for him. Present my compliments to Michael. I shall have the honor of writing to you whenever the opportunity presents itself, as you seem to desire it. Please let me hear from you, and send me whatever news you receive from your dear son. I shall be stationed but eighty leagues from Kourou.

I have the honor, etc.,

BESSOU, of the Society of Jesus,
Missionary in Cayenne.

No. 21.

(Translation.)

FATHER NICHOLAS DE GONNOR TO FATHER——

REVEREND FATHER,——P.C.

Several reasons have induced me to write you this letter: First, to assure you that I have always borne for your reverence an esteem bordering on veneration, and that my respect and devotedness for you personally are beyond expression. I have more than once reproached myself with not having sooner given you some token of my sentiments in this respect, and for having deferred the accomplishing of this duty. I wish now to express my lasting gratitude for your kindness to me on many occasions, especially while I was an inmate of the seminary of Luçon, which you governed for so long a time with as much wisdom as success.

Another reason for writing you is to beg you to break as gently as possible to Father Aulneau's mother the news of the death of her dear son, who, we have learnt but lately, was massacred last May by a party of wandering Indians, called the Sioux of the Prairies, while he was journeying from his own to another mission, with the intention of going to confession and of seeking advice on troubles to which his extreme delicacy of conscience had given rise. He is universally regretted by both the members of the Society and by seculars, for he was universally esteemed.

Last year, he preached during the Carnival at Quebec, to the great satisfaction of all, those who were not able to attend forming their judgment of him from the testimony of those who were present. The crowd who followed eagerly his sermons were outspoken in their praise.

Shortly after, he underwent his fourth year examination in Theology with ease and all possible success. It was then that he was named to take charge of the most remote and consequently the hardest and the most utterly destitute of all human resources among the various missions of Canada, so much so that during the preceding years two or three persons had died there of hunger.

He felt a great repugnance for this post, as he would have to go there alone, unaccompanied by any other missionary, there being too few to spare two for each mission, while some posts even were left vacant; he generously overcame this reluctance through zeal and a love of obedience, much to the admiration of those who knew how painful the sacrifice was; those, on the contrary who were ignorant of it fancied that he was delighted at the idea of discovering new regions.

In fine, Reverend Father, he was a true Jesuit and a truly apostolic man. I can speak with more certainty on this point than another, for, as you know, he was my pupil. From his first landing in Canada we became intimate friends, so that we had nothing hidden from each other. I deeply deplore his loss both as a missionary and as a friend. Everyone in the Mission is in great affliction at his demise, but no one as much as myself. What consoles me is the conviction that if God has cut short his career it is the sooner to crown his apostolic virtues. He even, it would seem, revealed to him that he would soon receive the reward of his toil, for the Father wrote to me but a fortnight before his death in these terms : " Continue, my dear Father, to pray God for me and recommend me to the Blessed Virgin ; I hope soon to finish my course, but dread lest I finish it badly."

He was surprised with twenty other Frenchmen, but it is not known how they were put to death. No premonitory sign of distrust on the part of the Indians was noticed, nor were the vict ims tortured, as they are wont to be when prisoners are taken in battle. It is conjec-tured that they were surprised while asleep, and received their death blow una wares. The heads of all were then severed from the bodies.

It is said, howe ver, that from the position in which the Father's body was found he must have been on his knees when he was decapitated, and one of the party who found him took possession of his *calotte*, remarking that poor as he was he would not part with it for a thousand crowns. Though we entertain no do ubts of his eternal happiness, we trust nevertheless that you will give him the benefit of the customary suffrages of the Society.

If you should yourself see the mother of the dear departed, or if you sho uld write to her, I beg of you to make her understand the share I bear with her in this deep affliction, and that my own grief is too great to allow my offering her any consolation otherwise than by beseeching the God of all comfort to bestow on her the graces she stands in need of to bear the weight of so heavy a blow. Allow me, Reverend Father, to close here, for my distress overwhelms me.

I am, with the most profound respect,

Reverend Father,

Your most humble and most obedient servant,

DE GONNOR, Jesuit,

Missionary of the Hurons at N.-D. de Lorette.

Convey, I beg you, the assurance of my great respect to all the Reverend Fathers of the Seminary, and in par-ticular to Father Bonin, Father Moreau and Father Pillex, as I am told they are with you, without forgetting Father Faure, if he be still there, as I am led to think. Kind regards also to the regents and other gentlemen of the house.

(N.B.—There is no date given, but the letter was evi-dently written in the summer of 1736.)

FATHER AULNEAU'S DEATH.

As wə have reached that point in the *Aulneau Letters* where the death of the saintly priest is recorded, it seems advisable to gather under one heading all that is known concerning the treacherous massacre which deprived the newly discovered regions of the great West of their most promising missionary, and threw back for an indefinite period the work of evangelizing the wandering tribes of the prairies and of the wilds bordering on the extreme western lakes.

All that Father Felix Martin, S.J., that indefatigable laborer in the field of historical research, could glean, thirty years ago, from various sources, is summed up in the short account found on a stray sheet among his notes, and which we here translate and place on record to save it from oblivion :

" We are not in possession of the details relating to Father Aulneau's family, education and vocation to the religious life.

" He came to Canada in 1730*, and six years subsequent to his arrival he was chosen to accompany an important expedition of discovery westward, undertaken by Monsieur de La Véranderie. The latter commanded a party of twenty determined men, one of his own sons being among the number.

" The explorers had reached the Lake of the Woods, and had landed on an island for their morning meal. Their camping fires, however, betrayed their presence to a band of Sioux warriors who were prowling about in the neighborhood.

" These Indians, notorious for their cruelty and for the implacable war they waged on all those who gave them

---

* The correct date of his arrival is, as we have seen, Aug. 12, 1734.

umbrage, resolved to attack the French. They stealthily landed on the island without attracting notice, and rushed upon the explorers who were off their guard. Many were pierced with arrows or were felled with the tomahawk. Some sought safety in flight only to perish in the waves. Father Aulneau, wounded by an arrow, fell upon his knees, when an Indian coming up behind him dealt him the death blow with his tomahawk.

"All the baggage was pillaged, but the Indians dared not touch the body of the missionary. Three weeks after the occurrence, a party of Indians of the Sault (*Sauteux*), passing by the spot, found his body unmutilated. Not being able to dig a grave for it, as the island was all rock, they raised over the body a cairn one or two *metres* in height.

"Mr. Belcourt, a missionary stationed at Pembina, in 1843, visited the place and saw the tumulus. He gathered on the very spot the tradition of the massacre from the lips of an Indian whose father had helped to prepare a sepulchre for the missionary."

Let us now add the only other existing versions of the event, wherein we shall find some few interesting incidents not mentioned in Father deGonnor's letter nor in Father Martin's account.

Father Lafitau, the same who had passed so many years at Sault St. Louis, writing from Paris to Father General, April 4, 1738, gives the following account of Father Aulneau's death :

.."Quod attinet ad Patrem Petrum Aulneau nihil novi praeterquam quod initio scriptum est. Secutus fuerat praefectum militum quem prorex Novae Franciae praeposuerat ut iter aperiret ad Mare Occiduum ex hac parte adhuc ignotum. Jamque pervenerat ad fontes fluvii Mississipi, et ultra progressus, sed quia mos est istorum ut suis ‚commodis plus quam communi bona vacent et

intenti sint, pulverem pyrium et alia id genus variis
nationibus vendiderat.

Istae offensae tali negotiationis genere hostibus profi-
cuo, occasionem sumpsere expeditionis cujusdam quam
praefectus destinarat filio suo expeditionis praeposito,
comite P. Aulneau, jam mortis suae praescio, uti ex litte-
ris suis constat.

Reipsa ipsos ex insidiis aggressi sunt barbari ac omnes
interemere. P. Petro Aulneau duobus pugionis ictibus
cofosso et capite amputato.''

Jos. Fr. Lafitau, S J.

Of this document, which is preserved in the archives
of the Gesù in Rome, we give the following translation :

" As to what relates to Father Aulneau, nothing more
has been learnt than what has already been written. He
had followed an officer whom the governor of New France
had commissioned to discover the way across the conti-
nent to the Western Ocean as yet unknown from this
side. He had reached the sources of the Mississippi and
had penetrated further west. But according to the custom
of adventurers of that class, who are alive to their own
interests which they consult rather than the common
weal, the party had, in barter, sold powder and other
munitions of war to the tribes they met with.

'' Some of the Indians, incensed at this species of traffic
at which their enemies gained an advantage, took occasion of an expedition this officer had planned and had
entrusted to his own son as leader, with Father Aulneau— who had a presentiment of his death, as his letters
attest—to accompany him.

" In fact, the savage band stole upon them unawares,
and slaughtered them all. Father Aulneau received two
thrusts of a knife, and was decapitated."

What might be called the official account of the massacre is preserved in the *Archives Coloniales de la Marine*,

*Paris.** This we have had carefully copied, and we append the following translation of it:

"Affair of the murder of 21 *voyageurs* which took place at the Lake of the Woods, in the month of June, 1736. A *voyageur*, Bourassa by name, relates that on June 3, 1736, having set out the fifth (of the band) from Fort St. Charles, at the Lake of the Woods, for Michilimakinac, met the following morning, just as he was about to push off from shore, thirty canoes manned by ninety or a hundred warriors, who surrounded and disarmed him and his companions, and plundered their stores. When they had learnt from him that under the curtain* of Monsieur de La Véranderie's Fort there were five or six wigwams of Cristinaux, against whom they had set out on the war-path, they released him, and departed with the intention of capturing the encampment. They told Bourassa, however, to wait for them, and at their return they would restore his arms. This he did not think advisable to do ; on the contrary, he hurried to Michilimakinac, while the Sioux, on their side, pushed on to Fort St. Charles, where they failed to find the five wigwams of Cristinaux who had decamped, so they retraced their steps.

"Meanwhile, twenty *voyageurs*, who had lately arrived from Lake Alepimigon, were on their way to Michilimakinac. At a day's journey from there (Lake Alepimigon?) they were met by that same band of Sioux, who massacred them all.

"Among the slain were the young Sieur de La Véranderie and Father Aulneau, the missionaiy.

"Their bodies were discovered and identified by a party of Frenchmen who passed by the same place a few days later. Their heads had been placed on robes of

---

* Nouvelle France, Vol. 16. Postes des pays de l'ouest, 1679-1759, C 1, Fol. 189.

* The *curtain* is the line of enclosure between two bastions.

beaver skin, and most of them with the scalp missing. The missionary was kneeling on one knee, an arrow in his side, a gaping wound in the breast, his left hand resting on the ground and his right hand raised. The Sieur La Véranderie was stretched on the ground, face downwards, his back all hacked with a knife; there was a large opening in his loins, and his headless trunk was decked out with garters and bracelets of pocupine quill.

" It will be only this year that we shall be in possession of the other particulars of this unfortunate affair.

"Some are of opinion that the Indians wished to wreak their vengeance more particularly on young La Véranderie, the son, who two years before had joined a war party of Cristinaux against the Sioux. It would appear that in the council he had been proclaimed leader. Be that as it may, the young man had desisted and had not taken part in the hostilities.

"According to Bourassa, the bulk of the attacking party was composed of the Prairie Sioux, of some Sioux of the Lakes and of Monsieur de La Ronde's post. The latter appeared well disposed towards the French ; perhaps they were overruled in the affair of the Sieur de La Véranderie's murder. If the Sioux of the lakes conspired with the Sioux of the Prairies to shoot the French, then there is much to be feared for the Sieur St. Pierre who is commandant at the post of the Sioux.* The Sioux nations are the fiercest of all the native tribes. They have been from time immemorial at war with the Cristinaux and the Assiniboels. These latter were originally from the same stock ; they speak very nearly the same language, and yet they are irreconcilable enemies. A circumstance which the same Bourassa reports is that the Sioux

---

* Fort Beauharnois, situated on Lake Pepin, about forty miles southeast of the present city of St. Paul, where Father Guignas was missionary and chaplain.

complained to him that the French supplied the Cristinaux with arms and ammunition. The Cristinaux might
as well complain of the French furnishing the Sioux with.
ammunition.

" The Sieur de La Véranderie writes that, grief-stricken·,
at the loss of his son, he intends placing himself at the -
head of the Cristinaux and Assiniboels, and of marching
against the Sioux (an extreme measure and not to be
recommended). He would do bet.er to agree to give up ·
his post of the Western Sea, or have another officer
appointed to relieve the Sieur de La Véranderie, who -
could undertake the task of conciliating all the tribes.''

The distance, even from the most western missions to
the scene of the massacre, was so great, and commun-
ications so often interrupted, that fully three years after
the disaster of the Lake of the Woods, the foregoing
meagre accounts received but slight amplification. In
1739, Father Du Jaunay, writing from Michilimakinac to
Madame Aulneau,* had little to add. "Concerning the
circumstances accompanying the death of your dear son,"
he' tells her, "here is what I have learnt from hearsay,
and some of my sources of information seem trustworthy.

" In the first place, the majority of the Indians implicated were averse to putting him to death. In the
second place, it was through sheer bravado that a crazy-
brained Indian set at naught the consequences which
held the others in awe.

" A third particular I have gathered is that scarcely
had the deed been perpetrated than a deafening clap of
thunder struck terror into the whole band. They fled
the spot, believing that Heaven was incensed at what
they had done.

" Finally, that the portable chapel† and, namely, the

---

* No. 29 of the Collection.

† *I.e.*, the small altar stone, sacred vessels and vestments, with whatever
else that is necessary for saying Mass while on the missions.

chalice, which was plundered, had fallen into the hands of a widowed squaw who had several grown up sons, the pride and wealth of the tribe. In a remarkably short lapse of time, all or nearly all of them perished in her sight. This she ascribed to the chalice, which her sons had given her; so she rid herself of it by throwing it into a river.

"This," concludes Father Du Jauuay, "is all I have been able to gather from the various accounts of the Indians. I met here with a native, who claimed to be a Sioux and to have been present at the massacre ; but on being warned that he was an impostor, I did not think it proper to question him, trusting to time to throw more light on the occurrence."

But more than a century and a half have added little or nothing to our knowledge of the main incidents of Father Aulneau's death.

No. 22.

(Translation.)

FATHER BESSOU TO MADAME AULNEAU.

From above the Falls of Oyapok Cayenne, S.A).

April 1, 1737.

Madam,

Lest I should fail in the promise I made of letting you hear from me, I now write in anticipation of the arrival of the King's vessels. I have not much to tell you. I have made but little progress in the language of the Pririous. It is difficult to learn. I have no helps, and but little hope of any in prospect, for in all the neighborhood there is but one slave who knows their language and who understands a little French—and what means have I of securing his services? They do not lend slaves without remuneration here. Meanwhile, I see with sorrow men die around me without being able in any way to help them to save their souls. It would be far more consoling if all those who die were little children, for then I could administer Holy Baptism. I have baptized four already, but as for the adults I can do nothing for them, nor shall I be able to succor them for a long time to come.

Our Indians speak with great volubility, in a low tone, and indistinctly, without articulating all the syllables of their words. Just as soon as my state of health allowed me, I began to compile a dictionary of their language. A dictionary of the *jargon* Galibi which I brought with me was of great assistance in the work. I have already set down a great number of words, but am not very far advanced for all that. What must be learnt next is the way they put their words together in speaking, for most of them do not understand unless the words are arranged in the phrase after their own fashion. This is not to be

7

wondered at, as they are very stupid and incapable of re-flection. Moreover, their profound ignorance of whatever may be said to them concerning our holy religion is of itself enough to prevent them from understanding. Con-sequently, it often happens that they tell us that they easily catch the words but do not comprehend our mean-ing.

There are about one hundred and fifty gathered togeth-er where I am, and fully one hundred more in the neigh-borhood. They all flocked in to the place of the mission, and when I arrived I was surprised to see so large a num-ber. They generally remain scattered, with the end, I fancy, of avoiding quarrels which might arise amongst themselves. We endeavor to bring them together, and it is even necessary to do so, not only that we may teach them Christianity, but also to see what passes among them, and to prevent them from having recourse to *Pyages* in whom they have great confidence.

These *Pyages* teach them that it is the devil who sends them sickness, and that they have the power of keeping him away. They are much respected among the natives, and this will prove one of the greatest obstacles to their conversion. Although the *Pyages* do not succeed in cur-ing them, they are infatuated with them, and especially the women.

I have already passed seven months among the Indians. Before reaching them I encountered many perils in my journey from Cayenne to Oyapok.

Our voyage lasted eight days, though we had but forty leagues of sea to traverse. Not later than the second night after setting out we lost our anchor, and on the mor-row our helm, precisely when we stood most in need of it, for there remained ten leagues of a rough sea to cross. The Indians who accompanied us made a new helm after the Indian fashion, but it was so unserviceable that we

were borne to and fro on the billows very much the same
as if we had no rudder. Several times the waves breaking over our canoe filled it, and we were on the point of
foundering had not about twenty of our Indians jumped
into the sea to lighten it and to hold the bow to wind-
ward. They are such expert swimmers that they managed to accomplish this feat and give time to the others to
bail out our boat.

We finally reached Fort Oyapok on the eighth day.
Father Fauque, with whom I had made this unpleasant
voyage, wished to keep me with him at Oyapok for a few
days. It was providential that I remained over, for, two
weeks after I was taken down with a continuous and ever
increasing fever. I thought for a while that I had reached
the term of all my journeyings, but our Lord deigned to
restore me partially to health.

I left on August 1st for my mission, which is about
thirty leagues from Fort Oyapok. I reached it in three
days in spite of the falls of this river which are frightful.
I am incapable of giving you an adequate idea of these
barriers to navigation. For any other but the natives of
the country it would have taken much longer to accomplish the journey. They are broken to this work, and are
marvelously skillful in hoisting the canoes over the rocks.

At night we camped in the woods, and luckily we had
no rain. It would not have been an additional comfort
in the condition in which I found myself. I had just
risen from a bed of sickness, and was suffering from a
light attack of slow fever which held me for a good two
months in a state of great weakness.

Thank God I have recovered my health. Beg our
Lord to give me the grace of making Him known to these
poor Indians, for whom He shed the last drop of His
blood.

Present my respects, I pray you, to M. l'Abbé Aluneau,

and with more warmth even to Father Aulneau when you write to him in Canada. I still cherish for him a whole-souled friendship. The distance which separates us has diminished it in nothing. I hope through the mercy of my Saviour to meet him in heaven, if we are to be deprived of the pleasure of meeting here on earth.

I have the honor to be with profound respect,

Madam,

Your most humble and obedient servant,

BESSOU, Jesuit

No. 23.

This letter, dated Poitiers, Sept. 18, 1737, from Father Magra, who was preparing for the foreign missions, to Madame Aulneau, contains no items of interest for the general reader.

No. 24.

(*Translation*)

FATHER BESSOU TO MADAME AULNEAU.

Address: Madame de la Touche Aulneau, veuve, au Moutier sur Lay, près Lnçon en Bas Poitou.

KOUROU, May 16, 1738.

MADAM,

The three letters you did me the honor to write— January 18, November 9 and December 26, 1737,—reached me safely. They gave me great pleasure. I was much edified at the generous way in which you received the news of the death of my dear friend, your son. The sacrifice you made on this occasion, by raising you above mere natural sentiment, is more than creditable and does honor to your Christian character and to your virtue. That you should have wept is praiseworthy, when

the tears you shed were those of joy and tender affection
at the death of a dearly beloved son who so well deserved
this appellation. Th e nature of his death would admit of
your shedding no others. Our greatest comfort in this
bere avement is the well grounded hope that at home in
God's glory he will not forget us here below.

I am never so grateful for the m any expressions of
kindness contained in your letters. If ever the occasion
present itself of showing you my gratitude, I shall
eagerly take advantage of it. Accept at least the expression of my good will, and do me the favor of believing
in it implicitly. Do not tire praying our Lord for me.
For my part, rest assured that I shall not forget you.

I have heard with satisfaction that our Father General
has made you a participant in the good works of the
Society. This affiliation gives me a new claim on your
pray ers and meritorious deeds ; and what you did before
for me through a motive of charity you owe me now, if I
may so express myself, through a motive of justice.

Since you are pleased to listen to what concerns me, I
shall set about giving you some of my news. I owe you
this on account of the interest you take in whatever
relates to our missions.

This year they are on the point of establishing three.
Our Superiors have destined me for one. They have
appointed Father Dayma to the mission of *St. Paul des
Saults*, in the Oyapok district, where I left him when I set
out from Cayenne. Along the Upper Oyapok, extending
inland, are a great many Indians of different tribes. But as
we intend to proceed step by step, we shall work to bring
about the conversion of all these natives by means of
those established along the banks of the river. Here are
the names of some of the native tribes : The Aquoquas,
the Ouages or, as they are called by some, the Ouaris,
the Taroupis and the Coussanis. The French and even

the Indians accuse the latter of eating human flesh. It is certain that the Coussanis have the reputation of being more ferocious than the other tribes who are in closer relations with the French. I noticed this myself when I made a journey into their country with Father Fauque, one of our missionaries. Of all the tribes settled along the Oyapok they are the furthest from the coast, and live not very far from the sources of the river.

We ascended another stream, the Ramopi; it is not inconsiderable, and flows into the Oyapok at a point about three days journey for St. Paul's mission. We paid a visit also to the Ouages, who dwell near its upper waters. We met on our way a party of Taroupis and Aquoquas, but their band was not numerous. Their villages are situated far up a number of little tributary streams impassable for our canoes. All the Indians we met, and they did not exceed in number five hundred, seemed well disposed and ready to settle in the spot chosen for the permanent mission, were we to take them at their word. Unfortunately, their fickle character leads me to think that it will take a long time to bring them together in spite of their promises.

Pray God that they may persevere in their present favorable mood, for they are to be pitied beyond measure. They do not seem to have the least idea of God, nor do they know what religion means. They are just like so many brute beasts, and their own idea is that they differ from the animal by their form only. They are wholly engrossed in the present, and have no thought and no fear of a future. Without my dwelling longer on this topic, you can already form a correct estimate of the satisfaction one may have in living among such beings. But however degraded and stupid they may be, a God shed His blood for their salvation. What a happiness, if, sustained by divine grace, our Lord should design to make use of me for the conversion of these poor unfortunate beings ! I do not despair of their con-version. Those who are gathered around St. Paul's mission were as barbarous as any of the others. They are beginning to be tamed, and a large proportion of the three hundred seemed to be inclined to become Christians. We instruct them, and they retain pretty well our lessons in the Christian doctrine ; but as we have to explain things of which they have had no conception, they as yet understand but little of the lessons imparted. We must hope that through God's mercy this understanding will come with time. This year we were counting upon baptizing a good number. I recommend them to your prayers.

Dear Michael's letter, which you enclosed to me, was a source of real pleasure. I am delighted at his choice, for he has entered a congregation highly estimable on many accounts. I congratulate you and I congratulate him for having chosen so well. Now you must be happy, for your youngest son has consecrated himself to God in fulfilment of your desires. This is another added to the sacrifices you have made to God. It is not often we see a family nearly all of whose members have devoted them-selves to the service of God. How consoling it must be for you to see the holy education you have given to your children bear such fruit ! I congratulate myself on having some share in the thoughts of a family singled out by Heaven for such blessings. I rely on your continuing to beg of God for me the graces I need to serve Him faith-fully. My respects, I pray you, to your dear *religieuse*. I have the honor to be very devotedly, Madam,

Your most humble and most obedient servant,

BESSOU, J.

. No. 25.

(Translation.

FATHER PIERRE DU JAUNAY TO MADAME AULNEAU.

Address : A mon Révérend Père—Le R. P. Recteur du Collège de la Compagnie de Jésus, à Fontenay, pour faire tenir à Madame la Veuve Aulneau,—Par Fontenay.

MADAM,

I beg you henceforth to look upon me as a son of yours, and as such to honor me with an interchange of letters, just as you would have written to him if God had not taken him from you. I am endeavoring to find out with some degree of certainty and with full particulars the circumstances of his death, and I hope that by next year I shall be able to communicate them to you. I send you the calotte he wore when he met with that precious death,—at least I shall beg our Fathers at Quebec, to be sure to send it to you. The sentiments redolent of tender piety contained in all your letters edify me beyond expression. I shall never forget that last interview you had with Father Aulneau, your dear son, and which you were kind enough to describe for me. Heaven grant that one day his dear brother, a Jesuit like himself, may follow him to the missions, but not to so early a death, for we are in too great need here of good laborers.

In union with your fervent prayers, I have the honor to be, madam,

Your very humble and very obedient servant,

P. DU JAUNAY,
Missionary of the Society of Jesus.

MICHILIMAKINA, Aug. 21, 1738.

No. 26.

FATHER LUC FRANÇOIS NAU TO MADAM AULNEAU.

Address: Mademoiselle de la Touche Aulneau, aux Moutiers sur le Nay.

MADAM AND VERY DEAR MOTHER,

I am at a loss to know in what spirit you received the letter I had the honor of writing you last year, and whether you might not have detected a vein of bitterness lurking in some of the expressions used. I acknowledge that I was wrong in wishing to place you on the defensive, though I did not think that I deserved the suspicions you seemed to have concerning me. It was for me to receive the reproof and not for me to administer it. I should have seen that your letter was dictated by a mother's heart, which is always apprehensive lest her children feel not as she does. Be this as it may, my dear mother, if any inconsiderate word should have escaped me, I beg you to accept my very humble apology, and I pray you attribute it wholly to my wish of conveying to you the sentiments of esteem and filial affection which I have always had in the past and shall ever have for you. I should be inconsolable were I conscious of having wounded you in any way.

I have not yet received the letters I am expecting from France; Father de la Bretonnière, who is at Quebec, will certainly bring them with him, but it will be too late for me to answer them before the sailing of the ships. I have no doubt but that you have written to me; and if your letter is not already at hand, I can find fault with the carelessness of my companion only, who forgets that by All Saints Day there will be no time left to write to France. So, my dear mother, it is impossible for me now to answer what you may have written. Perhaps you have asked me some little service that I can render next year only, for I am not able to devine your requests.

At all events, I am sure that you will be glad if I speak of our beloved martyr. His memory is held in benediction throughout the colony. He is invoked here as a powerful intercessor with God, and a great many persons affirm that they have received signal graces through his intercession. For myself in particular, I assure you that I have never invoked my holy friend without obtaining what I asked for. What a glorious privilege for you to have been the mother of a saint ! and what a consolation for us both to count on such a protector in heaven !

A party of Frenchmen had captured last autumn the murderer of our dear Father Aulneau, and intended to bring him to the French settlements to make him undergo the penalty he so well deserved ; but God reserved to Himself the punishment of his crime, not wishing that a death so precious in His sight should be avenged by men. Other heathen tribes rescued the Sioux prisoners from the hands of the French and sent them back to their homes.

Do not let the tardy delivery of your letter this year prevent your writing to me next year. And since you wish me to address you with all the freedom of a son who writes to a mother he cherishes and by whom he is cherished in return, allow me to lay bare to you my trifling needs. In our missions, beads and other objects of devotion are a great help when we wish to encourage the Indians to listen to us and to draw profit from our instructions. Could you not, through your dear daughter, the nun at Fontenay, have a little package of devotional articles, such as are constantly being made in religious communities, put by for me ? Father Bonin will see that everything that you would be kind enough to send reaches me safely, and you would thereby have a share in the good done among our Indians.

Every day I recommend you to our Lord, and I beg that you ask Him earnestly for my conversion.

I have the honor to remain most affectionately and respectfully, madam and kind mother, your very humble and obedient servant,

F. NAU, of the Soc. of Jesus.

SAULT ST. LOUIS, Oct. 10, 1738.

No. 27.

(*Translation.*)

REVEREND FATHER PIERRE DE LAUZON TO MADAM AULNEAU.

MADAM,

It is with feelings of profound gratitude that I now answer the courteous letter you did me the honor to write to me this year. I am all the more truly sensible of the marks of deference and respect you lavish on me, as I have done nothing to deserve them. It is true, I should like to have an opportunity of showing you how much I honor you.

The death of your dear son, so precious in God's sight, and which has made him a martyr of his zeal and charity, redounds greatly to your credit, owing to the generous way in which you offered the sacrifice of it to God. This alone, Madam, fills me with feelings of respect for you, which I cannot easily convey in terms. All my life, consequently, I shall entertain for you a well-grounded and most sincere esteem, and that, to all appearances, without the hope of ever meeting you save in heaven; but there, at least, through God's mercy, I trust I shall become well acquainted with you.

From esteem it will be allowed me to pass to real attachment. It is even a duty for me now, since, I should look upon you as a sister from the moment you were associated with the children of St. Ignatius. You deserved too well that privilege for Reverend Father General not to have granted it with alacrity and joy.

I send you, madam, something you will receive with great satisfaction and veneration : it is the calotte that our much beloved Father Aulneau wore when he was massacred. This is all that Father Du Jaunay has sent me. The French and Canadians wished to keep for themselves all else that belonged to him. I must add, and you must needs, madam, acquiesce, I do not send it to you entire, I have cut out of it a little scrap for myself, and I shall treasure it up carefully.

I address the package, together with my letter, to Father Bonin, to secure its faithful delivery. I recommend myself to your holy and fervent prayers, and I assure you I will not forget you in mine.

I have the honor to be, madam,-with the most profound respect and esteem,

Vour very humble and obedient servant,

DE LAUZON, Jesuit.

QUEBEC, Oct. 26, 1738.

No. 28.

(Translation).

FATHER NICOLAS DEGONNOR TO MADAM AULNEAU.

Address : Madame de la Touche Aulneau, Veuve, aux Moutiers sur le Hay.

MADAM,

It was with the greatest pleasure I received the letter you did me the honor to write. There was but one thing in it which did not gratify me, I mean the praise it contained to my address, for I do not deserve it, and your attributing virtues to me which I do not possess. On.

second thoughts, I conclude that I may take it all as a
kindly admonition given me, as God inspired you; and I
purpose hereafter, by becoming with God's help what you
fancy I am, to deserve the favorable consideration in
which you hold me.

I have now to inform you that through God's holy will
that I have come back across the seas to be treated for a
serious infirmity. I shall return next year to join once
more my dear neophytes. It is now ten days since I
landed at La Rochelle. Had the transaction of sóme
business with which my superiors charged me allowed, I
should have gone to Luçon, and even as far as Moutiers.
But what is deferred may yet be.

I am starting for Bordeaux, where I am to receive
medical treatment. I shall remain there until very near
the time I am to sail. I send you everything our Father
Superior gave me for you. It was addressed to Father
Bonin, but as he is no longer at Luçon, I have addressed
it, as you desired, to the Superior of the Seminary. I
am delighted at the act of justice done you by Reverend
Father General. I recommend myself earnestly to your
holy prayers, assuring you that you will not be forgotten
in mine, and beg to remain,

Most honored and dear Madam, most respectfully and
most devotedly

Your very obedient servant,

DEGONNOR, Jesuit.

LA ROCHELLE, Dec. 23rd, 1738.

(P.S.)—I am greatly obliged to you for the offers of your
kind services. I do not stand in need, thank God and
the charity of my superiors, of anything myself; but if
you wish to contribute any sum for the adornment of our
Church or for the relief of the poor of our mission, I shall
accept it; and, conformably to what you write me, I
shall let you knowhow to address your charities; at all

events, let it be understood that you are not to put your-self to the least inconvenience in the matter.

No. 29.

FATHER PIERRE DU JAUNAY TO MADAM AULNEAU.

MADAM AND VERY DEAR MOTHER,

It is late at night—and a dark one—that I set about answering your very gracious letter of the 6th of March last, but which I received only yesterday evening late. As this is the last opportunity I shall have this season, and as the bearer leaves in the morning, I prefer curtail-ing my sleep, though it is not altogether unneeded, than to be wanting in my duty as a son and not show you some mark of the lively gratitude I feel at your having adopted and substituted me for your illustrious and dear departed Father Aulneau; I shall do more,—for after the opening you gave me I shall write to the one who is now my dear brother by a two-fold title, I mean to the other Father Aulneau, your second son, the Jesuit. I shall leave nothing unsaid to induce him to join me out here on the mission ; so that, if Providence so ordains, we may go forward together, following in the blood-stained foot-prints of our dear brother, to conquer those sedentary tribes he was in quest of, and which were discovered this very year. It would not be, I know, without bright prospects of an abundant harvest of souls.

Help me, I beseech you, in this project, which to your great advantage will make of us either apostles or mar-tyrs, and perhaps both.

Concerning the circumstances accompanying the death of your son, here is what I have learnt from hearsay, and some of my sources of information seem trustworthy.

In the first place, the majority of the Indians implicated

were averse to putting him to death. In the second place, it was through sheer bravado that a crazy-brained Indian set at naught the consequences which held the others in awe.

A third particular I have gathered is that scarcely had the deed been perpetrated than a deafening peel of thunder struck terror into the whole band. They fled the spot, believing that Heaven was incensed at what they had done.

Finally, that the portable chapel, and, specifically, the chalice which was plundered, had fallen into the hands of a widowed squaw who had several grown up sons, the pride and wealth of the tribe. In a remarkably short lapse of time, all or nearly all of them perished in her sight. This she ascribed to the Chalice which her sons had given her, so she rid herself of it by throwing it into a river.

This is all I have been able to gather from various accounts of the Indians. I met here with a native, who claimed to be a Sioux, and to have been present at the massacre ; but on being warned that he was an imposter, I did not think it proper to question him, trusting to time to throw more light on the occurrence.

As for what concerns myself, the subject is so unworthy in every way that I cannot bring myself to speak of so loathsome a being. Do not expect anything from me on this score. It would require measureless efforts and whole peoples converted to Jesus Christ to cloak the malice and disgrace of but one of the sins of which I am guilty in God's sight, and I am all indolence and pusillanimity, a useless burden which the earth bears with reluctance and indignation. Let this avowal, I beseech you, excite your commiseration and pity, and make you more ardent than ever in praying God for me and for the forlorn tribes committed to my care.

Thanks for the alms you wish to give me. Through the great mercy of God and the more than maternal care of our dear mother, the Society, I stand in need of nothing. Assuredly I would sometimes wish for millions to induce these poor Indians around me who are always on the move, to adopt more sedentary habits. I really believe if they once settled down they could be brought to cling firmly to the faith. Meanwhile, and until, at God's inspiration, it pleases our King or some great personage endowed with the qualities of the mind and worldly wealth to show his munificence, it will be for you and me to send up our supplications from the foot of God's altars, and for me to rescue here a soul and there a household, now an infant and again a dying adult. It is even so with the affairs of God, and I would be happy if I devoted myself with fervor and fidelity to the accomplishment of such trifling labors. I have the honor to remain with all filial affection and respect, madam and most kind mother,

Your most humble and obedient servant,

P. DU JAUNAY,
Missionary of the Society of Jesus.

MICHILIMAKINA, Sept. 28, 1739.

No. 30.

(Translation.)

FATHER LUC FRANCOIS NAU TO MADAME AULNEAU.

MADEMOISELLE, DEAR MOTHER AND SISTER IN JESUS
CHRIST,

I received the lengthy and gracious letter you did me
the honor and pleasure to write to me this year, and with
it the box of beads and other objects of devotion which
your charity prompted you to send; but they reached
their destination only after I had written and despatched
my letters to France.   Father De La Bretonnière was the
cause of this delay.   He had gone down to Quebec to
purchase supplies for our mission, and from among the
things sent from France he picked out all that was
addressed to me to make sure of its safe delivery; but he
came back to Sault St. Louis only after the departure of
the ships.   He might have risked sending me on immediately my letters, to give me an opportunity of answering
them.   His excess of precaution was no gain for me, and
I bear him a little grudge, since it must have caused you
some anxiety.   Don't mind now, my dear mother; God
in His goodness, who knows my needs, ordained that I
should not be deprived of the outcome of your charity.

You desire me to make a candid statement of my
wants so as to supply them as best you can.   I did not
need this new proof of your kindness of heart to be
assured that I have found in you an affectionate, sympa-
thizing, beneficent, generous,—in a word, the best of
mothers.   I see also that you are convinced that I harbor for you in return all the sentiments of esteem, gratitude, respect, friendship and affection which a son whose
heart is in the right place should entertain for such a

8

mother. I have told you this over and over again, and I think that it is not necessary to come back on it.

As for my personal wants, I assure you that I am abundantly provided with everything a man in my vocation could desire. If the good God did not send me other crosses, I might well fear that the comforts of life would prove detrimental to my salvation. Consequently, I ask nothing for myself, as I am in need of nothing. But it is not so with my poor Indians, who stand in need of everything. I shall not be backward in begging for them, and charity in their behalf is never ill-advised. The beads and devotional articles that you have thus far sent have brought joy to the hearts of my poor Iroquois Whenever I distribute them, I make the recipients promise to pray for the one who in her charity helps them, and they never fail to do so. So you see, my dear mother, what an advantage it is for you to send them beads. My only recommendation, with regard to these beads, is that they be of six decades, and that the wire chain they are strung on be stronger. They have learnt here how to make scapulars, so that hereafter you need not send so many; but you might increase in proportion the number of beads and little crucifixes.

You have given me to understand that you would like to know what is being done here in Canada. I shall endeavor to satisfy you in a few words, for the messenger who is to convey my letter to Quebec is hurrying me, and it is the last chance I shall have this year.

The Sioux, who so ruthlessly massacred our beloved and amiable J. P. [Aulneau], have since then been so often defeated by the French that they have finally sued for peace. This has been concluded with them, as it is feared that we shall soon have war with our neighbors, the English.

M. de La Vérandrie has discovered a numerous nation

of pale-faced Indians thirty leagues from Fort St. Charles. Had it not been for the death of our dear martyr, these Indians, whom he is said to have met with during his expeditions, would already have received the light of the Gospel, for they are very gentle and amenable to reason.

An inexhaustible mine of copper has been discovered on the shores of Lake Superior, seven hundred leagues from here ; but the profits will never be very great, owing to the immense expense of transporting the copper.

The iron mines between Quebec and Montreal are more profitable, and begin to give good returns.

This last spring we sent out an army against the Chicachias, who three years ago burnt to death Father Senat.* Father de La Bretonnière accompanied (as chaplain) the three hundred Iroquois warriors of this village who take part in the war. Since then I have been alone in this mission, burdened with an inconceivable amount of work. Moreover, during a part of the summer, I was suffering from gout, while there were a number of sick persons to visit in the village. Not being able to walk, I was carried on a stretcher when I had to administer the Sacraments. I have not recovered altogether yet. Should the same amount of work continue for any great length of time, I could not hold out. About the feast of All-Saints I shall have assistance. Reverend Father De Lauzon, who is no longer Superior of the Mission, will come and resume his old position of Missionary of Sault St. Louis.

Father Bonin has written to me, giving me full particulars of the tribulations of our Fathers at Luçon It is a privilege of the Society to be persecuted ; but I think this is only a passing squall, which will soon expend itself when the new Bishop who is not yet acquainted with Ours begins to know us.

---

* See " Lettres Edifiantes " for an account of his death.

I congratulate you with all my heart, and I rejoice also for the Society at the fact that Reverend Father General has sent you letters of affiliation. It is an additional reason for me to remain with all the consideration, affection, devotedness and friendship possible,

My dear Mother and Sister in the Lord,

Your very humble and obedient servant,

NAU, of the Society of Jesus.

SAULT ST. LOUIS, Dec. 12, 1739.

No. 31.

(Translation.)

FATHER NICOLAS DEGONNOR TO MADAME AULNEAU.

MADAM,

I beg you to excuse me for not having written before my departure from France. It was certainly my intention —not to say my duty—for many reasons, and more especially to testify my gratitude for the very great and very delicate attentions received from you. When I reached La Rochelle after leaving your home, I found five of our missionaries awaiting me with impatience to have their things put in order, as they did not know how to go about it. Their difficulty was increased by the fact that our commissioner was a new hand, who had everything to learn, and who was just as anxious to see me about the preparations to make. After these preliminaries I had to accompany the missionaries to Rochefort, to see the Intendant and the Commander of the ship, a necessary ceremony for them. Scarcely had I them well off my hands when I received instructions to get ready myself for embarking. In a word, I was much put about. And this is the only reason for not doing what I should otherwise have done out of consideration for you.

The passage was pretty rough and disagreeable for
about fifty days. The rest of the time we had fair enough
weather. Thank God I met with no serious mishap. I
had even the happiness of saying mass every day, with
the exception of seven or eight days, when the gale was
too fierce and the sea too heavy. Finally, after a passage
of sixty-seven days, I landed in Quebec, where I found
our Fathers in good health. Father De Lauzon was yet
Superior, but his successor has recently received his
appointment. He also is from our province, and his name
is Father De St. Pé. Father De Lauzon is to return to
his Iroquois mission at Sault St. Louis to join Father
Nau, who is already there ; but it is doubtful how long the
latter will be able to remain, for his gout, which had ap·
parently left him, has returned again this year, paying
him very unwelcome visits. I am speaking from hear-say
only, no doubt he himself will inform you of the state
of his health.

I must not forget to impart a piece of news I heard on
my arrival at Quebec. It is that they have at last pushed
on as far as the nation whither it was intended your dear
son, the late Father Aulneau, should go ; and from reports
received, the tribe seems disposed to embrace the faith.
This bears out admirably what the Holy Fathers of the
early Church were wont to say : "The blood of martyrs
is the seed of Christians."

There is nothing else that I know of worth recording
in this letter. I recommend myself to your fervent pray·
ers, and I beg you to rest assured that I shall not forget
you in mine.

I am with respect and attachment, Madam, your most
humble and obedient servant,

DEGONNOR, Jesuit Missionary at Lorette.

P.S.—When you go to Luçon, please present my respects to all our Fathers. I recommend myself to their
Holy Sacrifices.

No. 32

(Translation.)

FATHER BESSOU TO MADAM AULNEAU.

KOUROU, April 24, 1740.

MADAM,

Some time ago I received all together three letters from you and one from our dear Michael. It is a great consolation to see that you do not forget me. Your letters are a real treat, and the expressions of affection with which they are replete can proceed only from a mother's heart. You confer no trifling honor by wishing to substitute me for your dear son, and I shall take good care not to refuse the adoption you propose ; I only wish that I deserved it some way. If the entertaining of the sentiments of a son entitle me to it, then I can safely say I deserve the distinction. Meanwhile, I repay you in full for your remembrance of me in your fervent prayers, and you can count on my not forgetting you at the Holy Sacrifice of the Mass.

All you tell me of our dear Michael is corroborated by his letter that I have just received. It abounds with exalted sentiments of piety. May God strengthen them more and more. I do not know, nor can I guess at the reasons which led the Bishop of Luçon to refuse him dimissory letters, but it is to be hoped that he will grant them in the end. It is a trial for our dear Michael, and will prove an occasion for further merit. I trust that it will not shake him in his vocation.

Father Baret's leaving was a surprise for me. I was well acquainted with him. God grant that he had good reasons for his act. Should you see him perchance, present my kind regards. I am glad to learn from your letter what post Monseigneur has given him. The news of Father La Johamé's death sensibly affected me. We both came from the same town, and he was one of Father

Aulneau's best friends, who had promised to go and join him in Madura. This is the second who has preceded me ; my own turn is coming. I had already heard since my arrival in these parts that Father La Johamé had met with much persecution ; may be his death is the result of it, but we shall learn more in time.

If you are apprized of any more particulars of your son's death, let me hear of them. I congratulate you on having received his calotte ; it is a precious relic that you must treasure greatly. We have nothing to fear in this country from the fury of savages. Our Indians are not very ferocious; quite the contrary—they are timid and retiring.

Since you are pleased with any little item of news relating to our mission in this country, I shall give you what little I have. I begin with that of the Kamopi, as it is one of those which are dearest to me. I wrote to you already that I had been obliged to leave that mission as Father d'Huberlant, who was stationed at Kourou, was not in good health. The Reverend Father Lombard sent him consequently to the Kamopi and me to the Kourou Mission. On reaching Oyapok, Father D'Huberlant fell sick, and was even at the point of death, so that his going to the mouth of the Kamopi river was necessarily delayed. However, he went there as soon as his health seemed somewhat improved. A short time after that he fell sick again, and was obliged to go to St. Paul's Mission. It was from thence he wrote me that he would return to his post about Easter-tide. It would seem that he is there already. At all events, from what he wrote me, the mission is in about the same state as when I left it,—that is, a certain number of Indians have gathered there, but they are not yet instructed in the mysteries of our holy religion, nor is there much prospect for some time to come of their receiving instruction, on account of the illness of their missionary which has hindered his learning their language.

Another Father had started a new mission among the Palissonis, but was obliged to abandon it, his health became so shattered; perhaps he will even have to return to France. He missed the King's vessel which was to bring out another missionary to replace him, but has with him yet all the letters she brought; this will be a very unpleasant affair for several. Yours would not have reached me had they not been sent by a merchantman from La Rochelle.

The missions of St. Paul of the Falls, of St. Joseph of Ouanari, and of St. Matthew of Sinamari have made a good start. Every day there are fresh conversions, as well as at Kourou, which is the earliest of the Indian missions here. Many more might be established, but there are no missionaries for them. Beg our Lord to send us apostolic laborers to rescue these numerous peoples from the darkness of ignorance, for they are willing to receive the mysteries of God.

In the letter I had the honor of writing you from Kourou I did not mention the danger I was exposed to in coming from Oyapok to Cayenne. I became aware of it only after the discovery was made that my travelling companions were a gang of criminals, and they acknowledged before the judge that they had discussed the expediency of throwing me into the sea. Our good God did not allow them to put their project into execution, for which I return Him thanks. This is another lease of life given me wherein to do penance. It will be a blessing if I do not abuse of this new grace, which is not the only one vouchsafed me. While journeying from Cayenne to Kourou, a squall capsized our craft while we were yet far out at sea. I made up my mind that I was lost, but I clung to the bottom of the boat as it did not sink. A party of fishermen espied our wreck and came to our rescue. I clambered into their boat while ours was being rowed ashore, where it was emptied and righted. I was none the worse except for the ducking and the cold, for I had ten leagues yet to go in my clothes which were wringing wet. As for my health, which you seem to think much impaired, it is not so bad as you fancy. It is not to say absolutely as robust as it was when I landed on these shores, but it holds out pretty well. I shall need all I have of it left, for there is a new language for me to learn, and this is not a trifling affair.

Reverend Father Lombard, with whom I have now the privilege of living, is often ailing, and each sick spell is of long duration. This is but the outcome of thirty years of toil among savages. Once more beseech God and His Holy Mo ther to grant me the graces necessary to make my service useful for myself and for the salvation of our Indians. This you owe me, both as a mother (by adoption) and as a sister (by affiliation to the Society). Charity, moreover, makes it a duty for you, for I am in absolute want of such help. Be assured that I do not forget you in the little I can do. Be assiduous in letting me hear from you ; you cannot imagine what a great pleasure you confer. I enclose a letter for our dear Michael. A respectful remembrance to all our reverend Fathers.

I remain, Madam, with profound respect, your most humble and obedient servant,

BESSOU, Jesuit.

No. 33.

(Translation.)

REV. FATHER PETER DU JAUNAY TO MADAM AULNEAU.

MY DEAR MOTHER,—The peace and love of Our Lord Jesus-Christ.

I have a very distinct recollection of having answered last autumn your letter of March 6th, 1739. I cannot, however, allow the present occasion to go by without sending some fresh token of remembrance this year also, as a dutiful son should do to a kind mother.

As I already gave you to understand, some years may elapse before we can gather any further particulars of the death of our beloved martyr. Meanwhile I herein enclose some papers which I found in his pocket-book, which will be acceptable, and from which I would part with regret in favor of any other save our common mother. To these I add a letter dated May 11, 1736, that is about three weeks before he was taken from us; it is an answer to one I had written him the preceding summer, the very next day after his departure. This he had put away in his pocket book among his most important papers. He was certainly far astray in the favorable opinion he had formed of me ; but it was, all the same, very gratifying for me to know that I stood so high in his friendship.

His letter to me is in Latin. It will be for you to have it translated by your confessor if he be one of Ours, or by some other Jesuit, on account of certain expressions dictated by humility, and which should not be taken literally but according to the phraseology of the Saints, otherwise they might disedify those who were not acquainted with him or who themselves might not be sufficiently schooled in Christian humility. Be careful also not to put too much faith in the expressions of esteem in which he held a poor wretched man like myself. His great charity blinded him in my case, and his ideas are totally changed since he is in the bosom of Light and Truth itself. He now looks upon me, and with reason, as anything but lovable, and really I scarcely know how I bear with myself when I enter seriously into myself. After all, whatever he may think of me, he knows that one day with the help of my God I may become what he is now ; nor do I for an instant doubt but that he is powerfully interceding to effect this. And when I think of it, I say to myself : "cheer up, toil, toil on to improve, and do not give up, the day of God's great and boundless mercies will dawn, and then.............."

Here are a few items of news which I flatter myself may interest you. Jesus, our bountiful King, has made use of me, all unworthy as I am, to enroll in His service, and I hope for ever, one Indian family. My main occupation this last winter was to instruct the father of this family. For more than ten years, and that without intermission, he has been suffering from paralysis, or rather from gout. On this very account I thought he would be more ready to receive the sublime lessons of the Cross. And, indeed, he entered into their spirit with such extraordinary zest, that I bless a thousand times our Lord, who works wonders where and how He pleases.

"Which would you prefer," I asked this neophyte one day, "to be restored to health or to remain as you are ?" After a few *provisos*, which bore on his submission to God's holy will and on a wish to work for His glory, he answered : "Remain as I am." "And why ?" I asked again. "Because any other road would be dangerous for me." And he added forthwith : "Because it is the one God chose whereby to lead me to the light ; because it is the one Jesus followed here below."

The spirit of God suggested to him on that occasion

motives, than which the most experienced preacher could find none more cogent to make a life of suffering acceptable. His peace and joy during the incessant and violent attacks of his painful disease, his zeal in instructing and in putting order to his household in the intervals when his sufferings abated somewhat, the earnestness with which he continues to make known God's holy word to his fellow-countrymen since their return from their winter's hunt, all conspire to make me hope that these admirable dispositions will have happy results in the propagation of our holy Faith. So may it be, and I recommend this intention to your prayers and to those of the devout souls with whom you are acquainted. I baptized him, his wife and his eldest daughter on the feast of the Epiphany, and on the morrow I married him according to the rites of Holy Church.

I conferred the Sacrament of Baptism on the remainder of his family, consisting of four others, on Holy Saturday. On Easter Tuesday, he, his wife and eldest daughter made their first communion. I administered at the same time Holy Communion to an old woman, an apostate who was brought back to a sense of her duty through his example, and who made a general confession of her whole life.

I know that many of the other Indians are shaken by his exhortations in behalf of our Holy Religion.

Once more beg our Lord not to allow these happy beginnings to prove abortive through any fault of mine. Alas ! I am quite capable of spoiling all.

This is all the news, my dear mother, I think worth while sending so far. As for my personal sorrows and regrets, they are occasioned by the consciousness that I am still a sinner and a great sinner, and by the reprehensible conduct of many of the French in these quarters, so that the great stumbling-block in the work of spreading the knowledge of the gospel comes from those of the

household of the Faith. This sadness is occasioned fur-
thermore by the thought of the multitude of souls going
to perdition, much through my own fault, alas ! and at
the sight even of the physical wretchedness of these Indians, the result in part of their own lack of foresight and
their wandering life, and in part of the avariciousness and
harshness of the whites, both of which are so inconceiv-
ably great that I dare not attempt to expatiate on them,
and so universal that they are beyond remedy. My sorrows are intensified by the knowledge of the great good to
be done, but which will not be accomplished in all likelihood for many a long day, for charity has grown so cold.

Many an earring, many a pearl necklace or brilliant
worn in France, many a wager lost at the gaming-table,
or many a fortune squandered in frivolous enjoyments
would be the means of winning over to Jesus Christ the
souls of the old and decrepit, the infirm, the fatherless,
and would draw permanently around me whole families
of unbelieving Indians, amongst whom religion would
have some chance of taking root. But no one will deign
to take part in the undying work of the Almighty, I
mean the building up of His Church, or, at all events, the
number is very small. So I beseech you again, pray for
me and for my wretched Indians.

PIERRE DU JAUNAY,

Missionary of the Society of Jesus.

MICHILIMAKINA, May 5th, 1740.

No. 34.

(*Translation.*)

FATHER LUKE FRANCIS NAU TO MADAM AULNEAU.

MY DEAR MOTHER AND SISTER IN JESUS CHRIST,

I address you thus since you do not wish me to call you
"Mademoiselle," so there is an end of it. I shall not
make use of that term again, seeing especially that it did
not express sufficiently the feelings of my heart for you,
nor those which I am persuaded you entertain for me.
Still, my dear mother, I think I detect in certain expressions of your letter a lurking doubt as to my affection
and sincere attachment, and I confess it causes me much
pain. Might it not have been the terms of respect I
made use of in my former letters that gave rise to this
doubt? But remember, my dear mother, that a son's
affection and love for his mother should not crowd out of
his heart the respect he owes her. Might it not also be
that I have never asked you anything for myself? It
would seem that this is one of the main reasons of your
suspicion, and I freely acknowledge that your suspicion
would be well grounded if I were in need of anything.
Once for all I protest that I do not stand in need of anything in my mission. Were the case otherwise, I am
sufficiently within reach of Quebec and Montreal, where
we have houses, to have anything I want sent to me. It
is true that our dear departed one, whose place you would
have me fill, would have acted differently ; but he was
far differently situated. He was in a region where every
human succor was wanting, while I am stationed in the
midst of French settlements, where I can procure all the
comforts of life. My own father who is still living, thank
God, and my brother who loves me with all his heart,

have this very year repeated the same offers as yourself—
and you can easily understand, my dear mother, that if I
were in any real straights I would not refuse their services, so think no more that I am wanting in confidence
in you, or am undutiful in any other way. Could you
but look into my heart, you would be satisfied with the
sentiments which animate it for the best and most con-
descending of mothers.

I think you must be satisfied at least with the freedom
and frankness with which I beg for my Indians. I refuse
nothing that is given for them, for their needs are not
imaginary, and there is no charity better directed than
that which helps to keep piety and devotion alive in the
hearts of these new Christians. It was with heartfelt
gratitude I received what you were kind enough to send
them this year; and when I distributed the beads and
other articles of devotion, they all promised to pray God
for you.

You should set great value, my dear mother, on these
prayers, for I dare assure you that they are agreeable to
God. The greater part of our Indian men and women
are remarkable for their innocence, and I know of many
who serve God as faithfully as He is served in the best
regulated religious communities. Continue, then, I beseech you, so useful a charity. Being affiliated to a society
that makes special profession of the Apostolic life, you
have a share, by your charities, in the works and merits
of their apostolate·

What you sent out for our church is very appropriate
and pretty, and I thank you with all my heart. However,
the pallas are much too small for our chalice. I am
deeply sensible of the kind civilities of sister Aulneau,
and I beg you to present her my compliments, and convey
to her the expression of my gratitude. She who belongs
to a community where they turn out such admirable

work could make something pretty for the church ; so I
take the liberty of asking her for a veil for the Blessed
Sacrament on Holy Thursday ; we have nothing sufficiently presentable for that august ceremony. Will that
please you, my dear mother? Could any son treat more
confidingly with a -mother whom he loves and by whom
he is loved?

But you ask me moreover to speak to you of my mission
and of my health, and I shall do so.

I counted much on Father De Lauzon, an accomplished
missionary, to relieve me considerably, but he has been
sick since All Saints, the time of his return to the mission, and so I am practically all alone in the village.
Our mission, which was not as large formerly as it is to-
day, kept five able-bodied missionaries busy. Judge then
of the amount of work we two invalids, Father De Lauzon
and myself, have to perform.

And yet I have, over and above, to attend to a French
parish of four hundred souls, more difficult to manage
than Indians ; and often to go on calls two or three leagues away over horrible roads in all kinds of weather.
The strain has weakened me considerably, and the gout
never relents even for a day. I had a terrible attack of
it this last summer, and for the nonce there was no mass
celebrated in the village, for Father De Lauzon was also
sick abed.

I should be so glad if Father Charles Aulneau would
come out to Canada. I could manage to have him remain with me, where he could be of more service than
among the newly discovered tribes who are not at all
friendly to us.

The King's vessel which came over to Canada this year
lost a great number of her crew and passengers through
some contagious disease. A Sulpician and a Jesuit Father were taken off, but the most serious loss was that of

our Bishop who fell a victim to the disease in the short space of two days. The letters and ship's cargo were scattered and pillaged. Providentially your letters and box reached here by a merchant-man.

The war on the Chicachias ended ignominiously for the French, who with the finest army ever set on foot in this country, and well provided with mortars and cannon, did not dare attack a rabble of savages; the Canadians alone and the Iroquois of our mission engaged the enemy, slew a number and took some prisoners, but were not in sufficient force to rout him completely. Father De La Bretonnière, who followed the expedition as chaplain, went back to France by way of the Mississippi. I think he will not return to Canada.

Farewell, my dear and kind mother, never forget before our Lord a son who is and will ever remain through life your most affectionate and dutiful son.

Believe me, my dear mother, your most humble and obedient servant.

NAU, OF THE SOCIETY OF JESUS.

SAULT ST. LOUIS, Oct. 8, 1740.

No. 35.

(*Translation.*)

FATHER NICHOLAS DEGONNOR TO MADAM AULNEAU.

Address: A Madame De la Touche Aulneau, aux Moutiers sur le Lay en Bas Poitou,—Par Luçon.

LORETTE, Oct. 27, 1740.

MADAM,

It was with no ordinary degree of pleasure that I received the very obliging letter you did me the honor to send me. I was not surprised at the courteous expressions or rather marks of friendship with which it abounds, though I would have you believe that I fully appreciate your kindness and am grateful for it all beyond expression.

You thank me for having called on you. True, it was more than I did for my own relatives, yet it is rather for me to offer you a thousand, thousand thanks for the hospitable reception you gave me.

I am pleased to learn that the merit of our dear Father Lafite has not been ignored, and am sure he will acquit himself of the duties of his office successfully and with becoming dignity. When you chance to see him, assure him of my respect and devotion.

You afforded me much pleasure when you informed me of what had taken place relative to your son, the member of St. Sulpice. As I take a deep interest in whatever concerns you, you need have no doubt as to my having shared as much as it was possible the joy you yourself felt on that occasion.

If I omitted to speak, in my last letter, of the mutual happiness of myself and neophytes on my return among them, it was either because I forgot to do so at the time, or because I thought it would not interest you particularly. When I landed, it was a surprise for me to find them waiting for me on the shore. There were great manifestations of joy, and they eagerly strove with each other to see who would carry what little luggage I had. But what gratified me the most was their telling me that, in spite of the oft repeated story that I was not to come back to them, they had never doubted my word. This was much to their credit, for the Indians are as changeable as the winds.

From the day I was left all alone to manage them, I have had no cause of complaint, and as to their dealings with me personally, I have reason to congratulate myself; but my real task is to lead them to Heaven, and at times I am afraid that they do not follow in the right road. Continue therefore to pray for them and for me, and rest assured that you will not be forgotten in our poor prayers. Recommend us also to those of all our Fathers in Luçon, and assure them of my affectionate remembrance.

I have the honor to be, dear Madam, very sincerely,

Your most humble and obedient servant,

DEGONNOR,

Jesuit Missionary at Lorette.

No. 36.

(*Translation.*)

FATHER JOHN BAPTIST DE SAINT PÉ TO MADAM AUL-NEAU.

Address: Madame la Veuve La Touche Aulneau, au Moutier sur le Lay, prez Luçon, à Luçon.

MADAM, MY DEAR SISTER IN JESUS CHRIST,

I can well give you this title since you are affiliated to the Society, whose child I have the honor to be,—but, to my confusion, a very unworthy one. As for you, madam, I know you have deserved this distinction much more by your virtues than by the sad event that determined the conferring of it. But why did you renew the painful recollection? True, it is always present to my mind, yet my grief became more poignant as I read your letter. I have the same grounds of hope as you, and even greater, having known what the dispositions of this dear son were almost at the moment of his death,—a death precious in the sight

of God, but a death of which I would fain lose the remembrance, the better to forget the incalculable loss we
have sustained of an evangelical worker full of zeal and
virtue, and endowed with every quality, capable of in-
spiring hopes of great achievements.

I do not here take into account my own personal loss
of a friend to whom I was deeply attached, and who
reciprocated my friendship, though we had known each
other but so short a time. But enough of this, for I see,
madam, that the affection of friendship may have its
moments of weakness to which maternal love is not exposed. Your love for him was intense, that I know from
other sources, but religion chastened it and eliminated
what was too human in it. I have not yet been able to
reach that point of perfection, so that I find myself as
deeply affected now as on the first day of my bereavement.

I fail, madam, to recognize myself in the too flattering picture others have limned of me. The color-
ing would be far different if I portrayed myself for you
from life. Nevertheless, I am willing to abide by the de-
cision of young Father Aulneau, if God heeds my wish
and sends him over here to take the place of his brother.
I am very desirous of seeing him come, perhaps too much
so; but all told, I see but that to fully make up for our
loss and bring consolation to myself. It will be, however,
as Providence wills it; the matter does not depend either
upon him or upon me. If I were sure that he would not
be averse to it, I would take action in other quarters,
with, I think, some result. In my present uncertainty, I
do not wish to complicate matters, nor ought I to risk it.
He is aware what my leanings are with regard to him;
this would be but a feeble inducement, if one at all. At all
events, I am quite persuaded that, go where he will, he
will always command the friendship and esteem of those
who will have dealings with him.

I have had delivered, madam, all the letters you sent
to my care, and I have no misgivings as to your receiving
answers from Fathers De Gonnor and Nau this very
year. As for Father Du Jaunay, that is another affair, he
is too far from here to be able to answer you before next
year.

I beseech our Lord to shower down on you His choicest
blessings. Pray to Him for me, I implore you; I need it
sorely on every account. It is in Him I have the honor
of remaining with due respect and devotion, madam,

Your most humble and obedient servant,

ST. Pé, of the S. OF J.

QUEBEC, Oct. 12, 1740.

NOTE.—To this letter, as found in the collection, a slip
of paper was fastened with a pin, and on it was written :
" The ship sailing for Canada will leave only at the end of
May."

I have the honor to be, your very humble servant,

J. VALOIS, *Jesuit.*

No. 37.

(Translation.)

FATHER BESSOU TO MADAM AULNEAU.

Address : Par Luçon—à Madame—Madame La Touche
Aulneau, veuve, au Moutiers sur Lays, Bas Poitou.

KOUROU, April 5th, 1741.

MADAM,

I have scarcely more than a moment to write you, if I
would avail myself of a chance departure for Cayenne ;
perhaps there will be no other before the sailing of the

King's vessel, and I should be much put out if it left
without a word of news from me.

I am very grateful for your kind remembrance of me;
and believe me, if my letters are any source of pleasure
for you, yours afford me not less satisfaction, nor could
you procure me a greater pleasure than by continuing to
let me hear from you from time to time.

I received with every feeling of gratitude the present
you sent me, and I look upon it as a relic; the recollection of your dear son who wore it will never be effaced
from my memory. I recall him now, that dear friend,
with a kind of veneration which makes me envy his lot.
Would that I had virtue enough to deserve a death similar to his. It is not that our Indians are not the kind to
perpetrate just such deeds. But recently we had a sad
enough proof of the fact. Two of them were principals
in a massacre, where it might be said barbarity was carried to excess. It would be too long, and I have not time
left to give you the particulars. You can easily imagine
the sorrow and vexation such a crime caused us, as much
on its own account as on account of the consequences
that may follow, and that would have followed already
had it not been for all the precautions we took.

The guilty ones have made off and have reached Suri-
nam, a dependency of the Dutch, who are sorry neighbors for the missions in these quarters, as the harm they
do is incalculable. Though the miscreants have fled, we
are not yet without apprehension. It is usual for the
savages to wreak their vengeance on the family of the
culprits when they cannot lay hands on the guilty ones
themselves. They have no regular code among them,
and think they have a right to administer justice themselves. Perhaps when we least expect it we will see some
tragic scene enacted; such men are capable of anything.
Not a few, however, among them give us great consola-

tion. Like variously graded wares elsewhere, there are some whose conduct is very gratifying, while others sadly exercise our patience. Beg our Lord to make us proficient in that virtue.

I am very glad to hear what you tell me about dear Michael. I congratulate both him and you, and I congratulate myself that he is honored with the dignity of the priesthood. I am sure he will not forget you in his Holy Sacrifices, and I flatter myself that he will give me a share in them too. The pious sentiments he seems to foster in his heart delight me, and you must yourself be much pleased to see him in that state of life to which you have every reason to believe God has called him.

I am very thankful for all the news you have taken such pains to send me. I receive but little now from France, where they are beginning to forget me. Three years have now gone by since I received any letters from Father Bonin. I should not be surprised at this, as you yourself receive none from him. Apparently his occupations leave him no time for letter-writing.

How sorry I was to hear of Rev. Father Richard's death. You were the first one to apprise me of it. What you tell me about Mr. Baret does not surprise me very much. He would have done much better, and the great number who have imitated him would have done better had they remained faithful to their vocation.

I regret exceedingly that Father Aulneau's health should be as frail as you say. When you write to him give him my compliments. He had promised me on my departure from France not to forget me, and that he would write from time to time and give me the news of our Province. The precarious state of his health or perhaps his occupations have no doubt prevented him from keeping his promise. I do not believe, however, that he forgets me in his prayers. Ask him for me for a

share in his Holy Sacrifices, for he must by this time
have been raised to the priesthood. Send me what news
you can concerning him since he will not or cannot write
himself.

Continue, if you please, to remember me before our
Lord, and communicate to me anything eventful about
our Fathers and about your own amiable household, for
I take a large share of interest in what concerns it.

I am with deep respect, madam,

Your most humble and obedient servant,

BESSOU,
Jesuit.

No. 38.

(*Translation.*)

FATHER PETER DU JAUNAY TO MADAM AULNEAU.

Address: Mademoiselle la Veuve La Touche Aulneau,
au Moutiers sur le Lay, près Luçon, Bas Poitou.

Recommandée au Rev. P. Procureur du Collège de la
Compagnie de Jésus à la Rochelle, pour la faire tenir au
directeur de la poste de Luçon.

A Luçon—Bas Poitou.

MY VERY DEAR MOTHER in the Lord, the peace and
eternal love of Jesus Christ,

It was only last autumn that I received your letter
under date of March 10th, 1740, and the return of spring
now bringing me the opportunity of answering it, I do so
with gladness of heart.

Dear mother, yes, and dear sister (for you see you are
both to me), your son, your brother enjoys in the midst of
tribulations of more than one sort the abundance of God's
consolations. He sees—for your injunction is that I
am to give you an account of whatever concerns him—

he sees little by little forming about him, through the very great mercy of our Saviour, loving members of Holy Church and worshippers of the true God. And although the culture of such tender shoots so recently transplanted requires much care and creates much apprehension, still he abounds and superabounds in joy to see that the work of God is being accomplished by means of so unfitting an instrument. Beg the Almighty to pour out a copious blessing on these very small beginnings.

I passed the winter with Father De La Morinie, who perhaps is an acquaintance of yours. Our main occupation was to serve God, to work for our salvation and for the salvation of the Indians Providence had detained in our neighborhood. Second to this, I busied myself teaching my companion the Ottawa language and perfecting myself in the same.

On the 14th of April, I started from here on the ice for a place called Sault Ste. Marie so as to help the Christian Indians who had passed the winter there to perform their Easter duty.* This journey, my dear mother, was not without its little crosses, but it had also its consolations. I was back here at my post only on the 18th of this month, where I learnt a most distressing piece of news. Last summer a little slave had been given me, seven or eight years old, belonging to the nation Providence had made use of to bring the career of dear Father Aulneau to a close. Already he had mastered his prayers and catechism, and I only awaited the moment when the lessons I had been striving to impart would have penetrated deep into his heart that I might baptize him. This I counted upon doing the coming year at Easter. On April 25, the feast of St. Mark, during my absence, he disappeared, and in spite of all the searches for him that have since been made no trace of him has been discovered.

---

* In 1741 Easter fell on April 2nd.

This blow overwhelms me, my dear mother, and if our good God in ways known to Him alone, and which are inexplicable for me, had not, in answer to my prayers, comforted me in His goodness, I should never again have known on earth what joy was.

I think you must be pleased with me, my dear sister and mother; for none other would I enter into all the particulars I now disclose to you ; my sorrows, my consolations, my occupations, all are laid bare to you. Have I not learnt how to be a son and a brother, a second Father Aulneau ?

I have not received a letter from his dear brother, but when you write to him assure him all the same of my kindly feelings.

I have the honor to be in union with your prayers, my dear mother and sister, your most humble and obedient servant, son and brother,

P. Du Jaunay,

Missionary of the Society of Jesus.

Michilimakinac, May 25, 1741.

No. 39.

(Translation.)

Father Luke Francis Nau to Madam Aulneau.

Sault St. Louis, Oct. 3, 1741.

Madam, my dear Mother and Sister in Jesus Christ,

I was delighted with the letter you did me the honor to write this year ; but I was also much pained to learn that you had been suffering from so long a sickness. Our good God had until then been sending you crosses bur-densome and very difficult to carry, and though you

made a pious use of them all He did not find you sufficiently chastened nor worthy of Him.   He now smites
you in your own person like another Job; blessed be His
holy name ! I am firmly convinced that the way you bore
this personal affliction will have drawn down upon you
new graces, increased your merits in Our Lord's sight,
and greatly enriched the crown He has prepared for you
in heaven.

From an earthly point of view I can but grieve at the
impairing of your health ; but looking upon it in a super-
natural light, I bless our good God for the new trials in
the midst of which He places you, and this, on account of
the profit you draw from them for your perfection.

My dear mother, do not take it to heart if you have
not been able to send me anything this year. What is
postponed is not lost. The poor Indians may be incon-
venienced a little for a year, but you will still have all the
merit of your good intentions.   When I ask you for
charity for my Iroquois it is always with the understanding that it can easily be done and without inconveni-
encing yourself; for if I thought that it would put you
out the least in the world, I should be the first to beseech
you not to send them anything.

A dutiful son ought to keep nothing that concerns him
from a fond mother whom he holds dear and by whom he
is loved.   I shall tell you therefore that as this winter has
been the longest and the most rigorous for Canada in the
memory of man, I have naturally been more troubled by
the gout than in preceding years. I am still confined to
my room,—in fact, I am not able to move a foot. Just
imagine my perplexity being practically alone in the mission, for Father de Lauzon is at Quebec, and the third
assistant missionary*, who has been only four days here,

*John Baptist Tournois, born at Orchies, Flanders, Jan. 1, 1710 ;
entered the Society at Tournay, Sept. 27, 1727 ; embarked for Canada
in April, 1741 ; made his solemn profession at Sault St. Louis Nov.
10, 1743, and returned to Europe in 1750 or 1751.

and not understanding a word of Iroquois, can do nothing for the Indians.

Painful as my infirmity is, I am beginning to get used to it, but throughout the winter I have been troubled by another kind of sickness, which, though not painful, gives me greater cause for apprehension than the gout. I suffer from vertigo; it has made me make more than one perilous leap, and may end by my breaking my neck. They have tried many remedies on me, which have done me some good but have not effected a perfect cure. At times I am seized with a sudden uncontrollable fear, which prevents my being left alone anywhere. Pray God, my dear mother, that He may deliver me from this evil, or at least that I become not quite useless among my Indians.

The Chicachias continue to burn all the French who fall into their hands. The English, who are settled among them, incite them to this barbarous practice, and often take part in tormenting the French more cruelly. Our Indians are always at war with the Chicachias, and from time to time they bring in a good number of slaves; but instead of retaliating by burning them at the stake, they adopt them in the village, instruct them in the mysteries of religion, and by holy baptism place them in a way of reaching heaven.

By this means our mission increases greatly every year, as well as by whole families coming from a distance who willingly settle down among us.

The care of the sick, settling the quarrels of the Indians, and all the other affairs of the village, which must needs be seen to by the missionaries, keep us so busy that it is sometimes far into the night before our breviary is said or our other prayers attended to.

The Flemish Jesuit, whom Father de Saint Pé had the kindness to send us, will be able only after a year to be of some service. By that time he will have acquired some knowledge of the language. To do all the work to be done would require a more robust constitution than mine. Ask our Lord to give me the strength I need, and be assured of the esteem, affection and filial respect with which I have the honor to remain,

My very dear mother,

Your most humble and most obedient servant and son,

F. NAU, of the Society of Jesus.

No. 40.

(Translation.)

FATHER JOHN BAPTIST DE ST. PÉ TO MADAM AULNEAU.

QUEBEC, Oct. 15, 1741.

Madam, and very dear sister,

Since this latter appellation is so acceptable, it is a pleasure for me to make use of it ; and despite anything you may say to the contrary, what I know from other sources, and the very way you express yourself, convince me that you are already, and that you will continue to become, more and more a worthy daughter of the Society. Would to God that after thirty-eight years elapsed this very day since I entered I could flatter myself that I was her worthy son. But alas ! my dear sister, how far am I not from it. It is for you and for me to strive to attain it, and it is the work of a life-time. Pray for me as I certainly do so for you.

I count always on dear Father Aulneau. A Jesuit who came over this year to us, and who, passing through Poitiers, saw him, has increased my longing to have him with us. He is a saint, not to speak of his other qualities, and consequently he is just what we need. A kind word from me, madam, please, when you write to him.

I have a letter from Father Du Jaunay, in answer evidently to yours of last year. By this time he must have received yours of this year, but he can answer it only a twelvemonth hence, and so on for the future.

As for Father DeGonnor and Father Nau, they are near enough to receive yours and answer them the same year, The latter, doubtless, will soon send me the one intended for you, which I shall enclose with Father Du Jaunay's. They will make amends for the brevity of the present one.

As a rule my letters are short, for my time is much taken up with a multiplicity of affairs, so that I have barely the leisure to renew the assurance of the respect and attachment with which, madam and dear sister, I remain,

Your most humble and obedient servant,

St. Pé, of the Soc. of Jesus·

(P.S.) Oct. 28.—There is no sign yet of Father Nau's letter.

No. 41.

(Translation.)

FATHER NICOLAS DEGONNOR TO MADAM AULNEAU.

Address : Mademoiselle Aulneau Au Moutiers sur le Lay près de Luçon, en Bas Poitou—Recommandé au R. P. Tavols de la Comp. de Jesus.

MADAM and very dear Sister—The peace of our Lord.

I should be much mortified if every year I did not receive some affectionate word from you. You may imagine then how much pleasure your letters afford me. I thank you with all my heart, and beg you to continue to give me this consolation. It was also with much satisfaction that I received news of your son, the Sulpician. I do not express a wish for him to come out here; but should his zeal ever lead him this far, you may assure him that he will ever find in me one wholly devoted to him, especially for your sake, and that on every occasion I should delight in showing him my affection for you. Since these are my sentiments, it is for you to contrive some opportunity for me to convince you of their sincerity. See, now, if there be nothing in these regions that you might fancy.

I regret not being able to write at greater length at present, as I have many other letters to send, and I must be getting back to my mission.

Persevere in your good prayers for me, and be assured that you will never be forgotten in mine. With all possible respect and attachment, I remain, Madam,

Your most humble and obedient servant,

DEGONNOR, Jesuit Missionary of Lorette.

QUEBEC, Oct. 10, 1741.

No. 42.

(*Translation.*)

Father Nicholas Degonnor to Madame Aulneau; address Mademoiselle Aulneau au Moutiers sur le Lay, près de Luçon, en Bas Poitou. Recommandé au R. P. Procureur du Collège à LaRochelle.

LORETTE, April 23, 1742.

I have read over and over again, my very dear sister in Jesus Christ, the kind and edifying letter you did me the honor to write to me. None could be more sensible of all the marks of friendship you bestow than I am, and be assured that I am really grateful, and that I shall never

forget all the kindness you have lavished on me. Please
continue to pray for me and my poor Indians.

This year I have been in utter desolation at seeing them
suffer from hunger, without being able to come to their
relief, not precisely for want of money, but on account of
the scarcity of wheat which failed to realize the bright
anticipations of the early summer. And what actually
afflicts me still more is that we are threatened throughout
the land with a famine more dreadful than that of last
year.

Before the grain began to ripen, worms attacked nearly
every ear, and devoured most of it, or rather they ate away
the kernel and left but the shell.

My Indians, all the same, will gather a little more Indian corn than last year, but their lands are so poor that the
harvest supplies their wants for but half the year at most.
The evil is diminished by half when there is European
wheat, and I am able to buy it at wholesale and deal it
out to them in small quantities, allowing them to pay me
when they can, which they do pretty faithfully when they
are able to earn a little.

But when I am not able to help them this way, they are
obliged to scatter right and left to find food, which
is prejudicial in no slight degree to their spiritual interests.
For, as you know, sanctity is rarely acquired by travelling
about. I must needs give my consent to it rather than
see them perish with hunger.

I deeply sympathize with our Fathers at Luçon ; when
you chance to meet them, remember me kindly to them,
and to Rev. Father Lafite more particularly. I was all the
more surprised at what you told me about him, as when I
was in France, His Lordship entertained a very high opin
ion of him.

We are here in a state of expectancy. We have a new
bishop, who seems to be kind and zealous; but they say
that he is strongly prejudiced against religious in general.

He came to my mission last year almost immediately after landing in the country, and seemed well pleased with the reception I gave him, and every time I have had occasion to meet him since, he has showed me much kindness.

I am not anxious to see your son, the Sulpician, come over to this country because the climate is not at all favorable for those who suffer in the least from weakness of the lungs. I have good reason to know that he would soon express his dissatisfaction at the change. You say nothing in your letter about your other son, the Jesuit : where is he and what is he doing ? For him, if, following the inspiration from God, he should come and join us here, I should be delighted to see him ; but unless it be God's own doing, I should not wish to see even him among us.

Before concluding, let me make one request : gather and send out to me and to our Fathers at the Quebec College as much porret seed as you can from your own garden, or from any where else you may find it, for in Canada this seed very seldom ripens.

I recommend myself very earnestly to your pious prayers, assuring you in turn that you will not be forgotten in mine.

Yours, with the sincerest friendship and respect,

DEGONNOR, Jesuit Missionnary at Lorette.

10

No 43.

(*Translation*.)

FATHER BESSOU TO MADAME AULNEAU.

Address : La Rochelle par Luçon à Madame de la Touche Aulneau, veuve, au Moutiers sur Lais, Bas Poitou.

KOUROU (South America), May 7, 1742.

MADAM,

It is a long time since I received your letter of September 7th. last. It was a source of renewed pleasure for me, and to receive news from you will always be a great satisfaction. You can do nothing to please me more than to write to me from time to time. I feel very grateful for the friendly feelings you express, and beg you to persevere in them, and to pray God for my poor Indians and for myself who stand more in need of your prayers than any other.

If you should ever hear anything more about the death of my dear friend, your son, I most earnestly entreat you to make it known to me. You know well what a keen interest I take in whatever concerns him.

Your dear Michael corresponds with me. He is still the same. What a comfort for you to be blessed with children of their character, all fulfilling their duties according to their calling. I am faithful in answering him, and shall be always delighted to have news from him. As for Father Aulneau, I have had no news from *him*. His occupations, very likely, leave him no time to write to me. I shall not complain, provided he does not forget me at the Holy Sacrifice ; indeed, I am confident that sometimes he makes a *memento* for me at the altar.

I am exceedingly obliged for all the pains you have taken to send me word of what is going on, and I beg you to continue to keep me informed of whatever occurs.

Father Faye, as I already stated, has been transferred to another mission, and to all appearances it will be some time before he returns to his own province. I hope he will always succeed well wherever he goes. He is an amiable man, as you know, and was very much attached to our dear departed missionary.

We lived under the same roof at Rochelle and Poitiers.

God be blessed for what you tell me about Luçon, for He can draw glory from all. It is to be hoped things will change, and meanwhile we must submit to our Lord's holy will.

What you tell me about Mr. Baret does not surprise me much. He abandoned the state of life he had chosen to try another, wherein he finds much more that is distasteful. It is what generally awaits those who have not been faithful to their vocation, and yet it is not an uncommon occurrence. They seek freedom, and meet with many deceptions.

You ask for an account of what concerns myself. Things are very much as usual. I am at present in charge of a mission which does not necessitate journeys as long as those I had to undertake where I was before. That mission was just at its inception, and I had to move about a great deal to perfect its formation. Where I now am, though the journeys are not so long, they are nevertheless far more trying for me. My stomach rebels when I attempt to journey by sea in small canoes; but this is sometimes necessary. Once when I tried to shun the trip by water I paid dearly for the experiment. I had been asked to go and hear the confession of a sick person five leagues away. I chose to go by land, on foot, rather than take to the sea. The going was easy enough, for the tide was out, but on my way home the incoming tide forced me off the beach, so that I had to walk nearly all the time on the muddy and soggy shore. This reduced

me to such a state of exhaustion that more than once I
thought I would stick fast. I finally managed to pull
through a little before nightfall. A severe attack of
dysentery was the immediate result, followed the next
morning by hemorrhage and violent tenesmus. As a
crowning misery, I suffered agony from a toothache. I
was laid up for a fortnight with a serious illness, but am
now pretty well restored to health.

I have gone into all these particulars because you insist
upon my keeping nothing from you which concerns myself. Shortly before the incident related above, I met
with another mishap, but followed by less serious results.
It was another sick-call, and at night. I had to pass
through a thicket to reach the horse they had sent me.
Providentially I had provided myself with a small lantern,
and it was well I had. I was walking on in front to light
the way for two negroes, one of whom carried my bed and
the other my portative chapel. I heard an unusual
sound. I looked more carefully ahead, and there, right
in the roadway, which could scarcely be narrower, I saw
a wriggling heap of something. It was a serpent "*à
grappe*," the most venomous that infests these regions,
whose bite is fatal if not instantly attended to. It was as
thick as a child's thigh. I thought at first that it was an
adder, and it was preparing to coil for a spring. I had a
thick stick cut at once with which it was despatched. It
measured about twelve feet in length.

On my way back from the sick-call, my horse sank in
a quagmire. Forthwith I dismounted, but in its struggles
to free itself, the beast's hoof came down on my ankle,
and in rising the haunch struck me in the chest and
stretched me in the mire. I was in sorry plight, as
you can easily fancy. I escaped, however, with a sprain
and a good daubing from head to foot.

Our Indians are very much the same, which means

that, for the most part, they are good Christians, less addicted to vice than the negroes, and than many even of the French ; albeit, some stray one may relapse into his primitive savage state, or return from a trip to the Dutch settlements a perverted Indian.

There, Madam, is all I have leisure to communicate to you at present. Once more I beg you to remember me in your fervent prayers, and to ask for me from our Lord those graces I need to work with fruit for the sanctification of the Indians and for my own. Rest assured that I shall not forget you, and shall ever remain with respect and sincere affection in Our Lord,

Madam, your most humble and obedient servant,

BESSOU, of the Soc. of Jesus.

No. 44.

(Translation.)

FATHER LUKE FRANCIS NAU TO MADAME AULNEAU.

Address : Mademoiselle de La Touche Aulneau—Près Luçon - Aux Moutiers sur le Lay.

QUEBEC, SEPT. 28, 1742.

MADEMOISELLE, my very dear Mother and Sister in J. C.

Pressing business and sorrow, by which I am overcome, do not permit of my writing to you at as great a length as I should desire. The death of our dear Father De Lauzon, the best friend I had in Canada, which occured at Quebec on the 5th. of this month, has necessitated my coming down here in haste to gather up the remnants of our little fortune, and to settle the business of which the dear departed had charge. I reached Quebec quite sick two days ago, and the King's ship sails the day after to-morrow. Judge yourself if, in my affliction and trouble, I am able to commune with you as long as I should have wished. Pity me, my very dear Mother ; pray our Lord to bear me up and to give me the grace of filling, according to His desires, the place of superior at Sault St. Louis, to which I have been appointed since the death of Father De Lauzon.

I thank you with all my heart for the beads you had the kindness to send me. If there be the least difficulty about the veil for the Chalice, don't give it a second thought. I have something more important on my mind now, for this year the best part of our revenue has been retrenched. All that now remains to us is a paltry five hundred *livres* of income, much too little for three missionaries. But God be blest, for if we are famished it will be for His glory. We did not come over here to seek for the comforts of life ; indeed they would be hard to find, especially these two last years when hardship has been extreme in Canada. Good bye, my very dear Mother. I would fill the four pages were it not for other pressing and indispensable affairs.

I remain, in union with your holy prayers, and with the feelings of a dutiful son, Mademoiselle and very dear Mother,

Your most humble and most obedient servant,

NAU, of the Soc. of Jesus.

No. 45.

(Translation.)

FATHER BESSOU TO MADAME AULNEAU.

Address : LaRochelle—A madame de la Touche Aulneau, veuve, aux Moûtiers sur le Lay près Luçon—Bas Poitou –A Luçon.

KOUROU, May 17, 1743.

MADAM,

Your letter of Dec. 12, 1742, was placed in my hands about a fortnight ago. It would be, I think, superfluous to tell you that it gave me much pleasure. I experience the same very sensible joy every time I hear from you.

You will allow me to upbraid you mildly. You have your son near you once more, your eldest at present, I mean; for I have learnt it through Father Aulneau's letters, and yet you never said a word to me about it. Do you fancy that I take so little interest in what concerns you, that you should not apprise me of this piece of good news? It is by the merest chance that I heard of it. Do me a little justice, and believe that whatever is of a nature to console you brings me consolation also. I congratulate you, madam, on the return of this dear child of yours; and may he now, by his presence, bring you as much joy as his absence did sorrow. Our Lord has deigned to compensate you for the sacrifice which you had so generously made Him of your other children. I give Him thanks and take part in your joy. Henceforth I trust that you will inform me of every occurrence relating to your own dear family. This, at least, is my desire and I ask it of you as a favor.

It is a long time now since you have spoken to me of your daughter, the *religieuse de la Foi;* I have not forgotten her. I would be very sorry to learn that she has forgotten me in her prayers, for it would be much to my detriment. Offer her my kind regards and recommend me to her fervent prayers.

Many thanks for all the other news you give me I read over with much satisfaction the reverend and dear Father Aulneau's letters. Their perusal makes me regret all the more that he would not or could not write to me since I came to these regions, though, when we took leave of each other, he promised to do so. His time is more usefully employed ; this at least consoles me.

I received a letter from our dear Michael, and it corroborates what you say of him, for it breathes piety in every line. You are a happy mother to have such children, faithful to the duties of their state of life, and not proving recreant to their vocation like so many others.

What you impart to me on this score afflicts me all the more as the faithlessness to their religious profession, of those you mention, has led to their falling away from the faith. This is very sad. When once we begin to separate ourselves from God to what lenghts are we not tempted to go, and how much have we not to fear ! To leave an order when we are convinced that we are not called to it is not an evil. There may be reasons for leaving it, but there can be none for embracing heresy. As for the Society, it is a great gain to be able to rid herself of members capable of such excessess. This will ever keep her firm in her faith and steadfast in her submission to her first pastors. The vanity of the heretic acknowledges no such blind submission, but the faithful glory in its practice. Our pastors are indeed our guides, and by following them we cannot go astray.

The announcement of the beatification of the Forty Martyrs is most consoling. I saw from afar the shores hallowed by their martyrdom. I mean the island of Palma of which we catch a glimpse on our way to this

country. Had the rough weather we encountered continued a little longer we should have put in to that port. I
should not have been sorry, for joyfully would I have
kissed those shores bathed with the blood of so illustrious
a band of missionaries on their way to America.

The aim of heretical zeal was not to propagate the faith,
but to cut short the career of those who longed to implant
it in heathen lands. Heresy endeavours to destroy, the
Church to build up. This feature of the Roman Catholic
Church has always distinguished her in the past, and
will continue to distinguish her in the future from
surrounding sects, and should make us cling to her
forever.

Our missions are getting on as usual, and continue to
gain adherents to the faith ; but we are always in dire
want of apostolic labourers. Five were to have come out
to us this year, but only one reached us. Death overtook
one at LaRochelle, sickness or some other cause detained
the others. And who knows when they will come now,
and if at all, it will always be too late.

We celebrated the jubilee this year, or to be more correct, the year gone by. This gave us no end of work. At
the feast of All Saints I went to Cayenne to help our
Fathers. I was yet in my convalescence after a tedious
sickness.

I drew on myself the indignation of certain persons,
who hurried to send off letters to the Court against me.
I have not taken the thing much to heart, and what I did
I should be ready to do over again if the same occasion
presented itself. I do not know what answers they have
received by the King's ship. If they are favourable to
them they will not leave me long in ignorance of their
contents. You see we are all the same Jesuits everywhere, since everywhere they make it a point to injure

us. God will find means to succour us, if He deems it best in His wisdom.

Do not grow weary, I pray you, in sending me news about yourself and whatever you may hear affecting the Society. You can do me no more acceptable favor unless it be to redouble your prayers to God in my behalf. It would be a real charity, for I have more need of prayers than any other. Believe me, I shall never forget you in my Holy Sacrifices.

Remember me kindly to Reverend Father Terreneuve. If I have time I shall drop him a line to renew the interchange of letters which at one time we had begun.

I am much pained to hear of Father Reveilland's weak state of health. Reverend Father Aulneau I shall not forget, as I also bear in mind all our reverend Fathers of Luçon and Fontenay.

I remain with the most sincere devotion and the most profound respect, Madam,

Your most humble and most obedient servant,

BESSOU, Jesuit.

— — — — —

No. 46.

(*Translation.*)

FATHER LUKE NAU TO MADAME AULNEAU.

Mademoiselle, very dear Mother and Sister in Jesus-Christ,

The consoling letter of April 28, which you were kind enough to write me, has at last reached its destination. For a long time I was apprehensive as to what would become of it and of the other letters from France sent to my address, for while I was already on my way to Quebec they were sent up to Montreal by a not very reliable messenger. But I have received it at last, that consoling letter, and it would be hard to tell you how much pleasure it afforded me.

How shall I thank you for the beautiful present you have sent to our impecunious church! It was for the embellishment of God's altars and for His own glory that you made the offering of this magnificent veil, Our Lord, consequently, will take it upon Himself to reward you; but I must add my own most heartfelt thanks for those many motives of consolation you suggest in view of my sufferings and sorrows. Often have I myself dwelt on these motives of consolation, and despite every endeavour I have been unable to sear up the heart's wound caused by Father De Lauzon's death. It still bleeds and will bleed afresh for many a day yet. Daily and hourly every object that meets my gaze reminds me of the loss I have sustained. I need all my faith to bear up under the weight of sorrow and anguish which oppresses my soul. I trust, however, that all you have had the kindness to write, my dear Mother, when well considered and pondered, will, with the healing hand of time, restore me to my former frame of mind.

I must confess, my very dear Mother, that the Good God has so afflicted me this year in my body, that had not all my other subjects of sorrow been so deeply graven in my heart and soul they would easily have passed unheeded.

Not to speak of the wretchedness resulting from a winter the most rigourous ever experienced in Canada, my attack of gout was more acute and lasted longer than any previously. I was not able to leave my room throughout all the cold season. It is only since the month of June that I have begun to enjoy tolerably good health; but even now not a day passes without my feeling some twinges of the gout. The evil has reached my knees, and I can make only half-genuflections, while there is every probability of its soon going higher, and that it will reach my chest ; then I shall have to pack up for the next world.

May God grant me the grace of bearing patiently and in a Christian spirit the violence of the pain, that it may be accepted as my purgatory upon earth.

I have another infirmity which, though it be not so painful, incommodes and worries me. My sight was not any too good when I came to Canada, but since my sojourn here the glare of light from the snow has so weakened my eyesight that the broad daylight becomes almost unbearable. I cannot, in winter, venture out without being immediately dazed and without losing myself, for I am unable to see my way ten steps ahead . I cannot distinguish a man from the trunk of a tree. By remaining in Canada a few years longer I foresee that I shall become totally blind, if the gout does not carry me off before then.

These were reasons cogent enough to determine me to ask to return to France, but Father Saint Pé, who has come back here as our superior, is unable to grant that request for want of missionaries. Should any new ones come out here next year they will be able to replace me, and then, my dear Mother, I shall have the happiness of seeing you.

My companion at Sault St. Louis is Father Tournois. He is a young Flemish Jesuit, well deserving and very affable. He is not proficient in the language yet, and I regret it the more.

In spite of the poverty of our mission we have managed to live, and have had palpable proof that God never forsakes those who trust in Him. Go on praying our Lord for me : I am in sore need of your prayers. I am mindful of·you every day at the holy altar.

I have the honour to be, with respect and devotedness, my very dear Mother,

Your most humble and obedient servant,

NAU, of the Soc. of Jesus.

Quebec, October 17, 1743.

No. 47.

(*Translation*)

FATHER DUBOIS TO MADAME AULNEAU.

Address : Mademoiselle La Touche Aulneau, en la Maison de Moutiers, près Luçon. A Luçon—Bas Poitou.

Mademoiselle,

I do not know if I had the honour of answering you previous to my departure. At all events, you will be glad to know that at last I have reached my destination and in excellent health, thank God. Our voyage lasted fifty-eight days, during fifteen of which I was laid up. The first tempests which we encountered were the only ones which inspired me with fear, and I commended my soul to God.

A little confidence in the Blessed Virgin, doubtless, will dispel many causes of apprehension in the future. But all the past must count for little now that I am at my journey's end. It remains for me to acquit myself of the task for which I came. Here more than elsewhere have we to labour, and, short of martyrdom, we have as much to suffer and to fear as if we were among savages. We escape the cruelty of human beings to be tortured by insects, and the frightful roads we travel, when we go on sick-calls two or three leagues off, bring us at every step face to face with death.

In other respects the country is a delightful one. The trees, all the year round, are laden with blossoms and fruits, and are of perennial verdure. The heat is excessive, and yet the poor pastor must climb, now on foot and anon on horseback, rugged heights to minister to the sick whom he often finds hale and hearty when he arrives. They have no pity on us.

The aspect of La Martinique may be best likened to a cluster of sugar-loaves crowded together. There is not in the whole island, for the space of a gun shot, an even stretch of land.

I am not certain what I shall have to do. So far, I have taken charge of the three parishes we have in the country, and I have performed all the functions of pastor, save that I have not celebrated any marriages.

Provisions are very much the same as in France, with the exception of butcher's meat which is as scarce as it is wretched. Everything, however, is extremely dear. Salt beef is sold at 15 or 20 *sols* a pound, a pullet for 6H, a capon 7H 10 d., a turkey 24H, a turkey-cock 30H, eggs 30 to 40 *sols* a dozen, a bottle of atrocious wine 30 *sols*, and all else in proportion. Fish is every bit as dear. *Grages* are eaten ; I brought myself to taste of the first I saw served up, but I ate sparingly, for the very thought of the thing was too much for me. Those great worms that in France are found in decayed trees are eaten here. I did not feel so much repugnance for these. Nevertheless, such things are esteemed as delicacies by the inhabitants of this country, who include also large snakes in their bill of fare. I saw one which I was told was small, though it was six feet long, this I refused to taste. And yet, I must accustom myself to these dishes, for if perchance we should run short of provisions, which are brought from Europe, we shall have to fall back on such like food or starve to death.

Sugar, coffee and chocolate are the only things raised

here. The negroes are fed on roots which are ground into
a kind of flour. This they eat without any seasoning.

I shall not write at greater length to-day, but shall
send before long a detailed account of what is to be found
in these regions; this the Reverend Father Lafite will
have the kindness to communicate to you. I shall request
him to do so.

Give me a little share in your pious prayers, we all
need it. I have the honour to be, with sincere attachment and respect, mademoiselle,

Your very humble and obedient servant,

DUBOIS, Jesuit.

Fort St. Peter, Island of La Martinique,
May 16, 1744.

You may direct your answers to Brother Vincent, at the
Professed House of Bordeaux. We are but fourteen priests
here and three brothers. I am not sure if you spoke to me
of Father Desbouge. He is Superior of Guadeloupe, which
is another island at some distance from this one.

No. 48.

(*Translation*)

FATHER CHARLES AULNEAU TO HIS MOTHER.

Address : A mademoiselle La Touche Aulneau—Aux
Moutiers sur le Lay.

My dearest Mother, the peace of Jesus-Christ,

I pray that your health may remain for a long time as
good as you assure me it is just now. With regard to my
own, thank God, I have nothing to add.

Reverend Father Michelain is very obliging to think
of me. He could not well think of another who esteems
and honours him more than I do. Have the kindness,

my dear Mother, to make known to him my sentiments, those more especially of gratitude for the gracious compliment he pays me in your letter.

Have you heard yet that Father Nau is now quartered at La Rochelle ? It is said he is to take charge of the seminary. If this be true, he becomes your close neighbour and our own, and doubtless, with God's help, he will, during the vacations, make his appearance for a few days at Moutiers and at Luçon.

In the shape of news all I send you this time, my dear Mother, is the copy of a letter from China. The information it contains cannot fail to be for you a source of pleasure and edification. You have as much right to know what is going on there as the Jesuits, since you do not take less interest than they in what concerns the Society and our missions more particularly.

The writer of this letter is Father Neuvialle a Jesuit of our province who entered about the same time as several of our Fathers of the Seminary. It is addressed to Mons. l'abbé d'Armagnac, who is most devoted to us, and who every year sends out to Father Neuvialle substantial help for his mission. The copy is not in my handwriting, as I had not time for that ; but I hope that you will not have more difficulty reading it than if I had transcribed it for you myself.

I bespeak a fair share of your prayers for our missionaries, for the new Christian centres wherein they labour, and for the heathens they are striving to convert ; nor will you be unmindful of a son who is full of sentiments of tender love for you, and who shall forever be, with the most profound respect, my dearest Mother,

Your most humble and obedient servant,

AULNEAU, of the Society of Jesus.

Luçon, April 4, 1745.